FIRST LOVE

A Young People's Guide to Sexual Information

Dr. Ruth Westheimer
and
Dr. Nathan Kravetz

D0907825

A Time Warner Company

*To my husband, Fred, my daughter, Miriam,
and my son, Joel.*

****

*To my wife, Evelyn and our children, Deborah and
Daniel.*

WARNER BOOKS EDITION

**Copyright © 1985 by Karola, Inc.
All rights reserved.**

Text illustrations copyright © 1985 by Frederick Porter

Warner Books, Inc.
1271 Avenue of the Americas
New York, N.Y. 10020

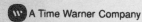 A Time Warner Company

Printed in the United States of America

First Printing: October, 1985

Reissued: August, 1987

10 9 8 7 6 5

CONTENTS

Dr. Ruth Westheimer, America's best-known psychosexual therapist, gives sound sexual guidance to thousands each week on her nationally syndicated radio show, *Sexually Speaking* and her cable television program, *Good Sex! with Dr. Ruth Westheimer*. Dr. Ruth received her doctorate in the Interdisciplinary Study of the Family from Columbia University and is an Adjunct Associate Professor at New York Hospital–Cornell University Medical Center in the well-known sex therapy teaching program led by Dr. Helen Singer Kaplan. She also leads a monthly seminar on adolescent sexuality at Brookdale Hospital in New York.

Dr. Nathan Kravetz is currently a Professor of Education at California State University, San Bernardino. He received his doctorate in education from UCLA and is professor emeritus at City University of New York. A Harvard University Fellow in Education who has been a teacher, principal, and counselor of young adolescents, Dr. Kravetz has developed sex education curriculums in both the U.S. and abroad. He is the author of numerous children's books as well as many professional articles on various aspects of education and is listed in *Who's Who in America*.

Acknowledgments

Thank you! to my family, teachers, colleagues and friends who have influenced my work and enriched my life with their friendship.

William Sweeney, M.D., Helen Singer Kaplan, M.D., Ph.D., Mildred Hope Witkin, Ph.D., Barbara Hogan, Ph.D., Harvey Gardner, Avi Feinglass, Joel Einleger, David Goslin, Ph.D., Hope Leichter, Ph.D., Stuart Cattell, John and Ginger Lollos, Larry Angelo, the staff of the NBC Young Adult Entertainment Network, WYNY Radio, KFI Radio, Lifetime Cable Network and the William Morris Agency, Susan Brown, Hank Barry, Frank Ciarkowski, Betty Elam, Jack Forest, M.D., Frederick Herman, Al Kaplan, Harold Koplewicz, M.D., Marga and Bill Kunreuther, Joanne and Pierre Lehu, Lou Lieberman, Ph.D., Rabbi Robert Lehman and Lani Lehman, Dale Ordes, Asa Ruskin, M.D., Francine Ruskin, Ed.D., Hannah Strauss, Arthur Snyder, M.D., Ira Sacker, M.D., Fred Silberman, John Silverman, and Fred Zeller.

Special thanks to Bernard Shir-Cliff, my editor, and Margery Schwartz, managing editor.

Introduction

Sex education is not a one-time event.

Fortunately many schools are now introducing sex education into their curricula. Even nursery schools incorporate information about conception and reproduction into the day-to-day learning activities of their preschoolers. I am in favor of educating our children about sexual matters right from the beginning. While naming body parts for an infant, the correct terms for the sexual organs should be included along with other parts of the anatomy. This provides a good foundation for further education as the child grows and more complex questions emerge. Sex education begins in infancy.

But contexts change and the teenager who has heard it all before now has reason to hear it all again. No matter how complete one's early sex education may have been, during adolescence there is a need for a refresher course with much greater elaboration of information and specificity of facts. It is well known that previously acquired information takes on new meanings when the reasons for knowing it are different. For youth, sex assumes a degree of importance that many adults do not fully appreciate. Need we be reminded that puberty means the attainment of sexual maturity? It is a time when physical and mental changes are accompanied by new and powerful urges as well as unfamiliar feelings and puzzling concerns.

Many people feel guilt and shame in connection with their sexual thoughts and behavior. Despite the claim that we have presumably been "liberated," many of our brightest minds remain filled with misinformation about sex. Since sexual acts are personal matters (sex organs are even referred to as "private parts"), correct information is often difficult to acquire. Some feel shy about revealing a lack of knowledge and therefore resist obtaining information. For others it may be impractical to call on a friend, parent, teacher, or physician each time a new concern or question arises.

In *First Love* you will find all the basics. In clear direct language, anatomy and sexual behavior are discussed fully. You will also find explanations for many common but less frequently discussed concerns, e.g. Can a virgin use a tampon? Is there something wrong if a male is unable to urinate with an erection?

But Dr. Ruth's book is more than a mere compendium of mechanics. Attitudes, values, and feelings are discussed throughout. Love, care, intimacy, and healthy relationships are stressed.

> The most satisfactory sex is generally agreed to be between people who have a sustained relationship—who have been together for some time and feel secure in each other's company. Casual sex, hastily agreed on between people who have just met or who have no real feeling for each other, is often a disappointing experience. Even when it is physically satisfactory, the lack of emotional closeness makes such sexual encounters rather saddening.

Clearly, *First Love* does not promote promiscuity and capricious sexual behavior. In a highly readable style, sensible information is conveyed to all who wish to know more. Parents will find it invaluable in preparing to offer information to their children. It is equally appropriate in more formal learning environments. It is especially useful and reassuring to those among us who are about to navigate unknown terrains. *First Love* is a reliable reference book upon which one can depend with confidence.

—Lawrence Balter, Ph.D.,

Professor of Educational Psychology, New York University

Author, *Dr. Balter's Child Sense,*

Program Host, *ABC TALKRADIO,*

Child Psychologist, *CBS-TV Morning News,*

Practicing Psychologist and Psychoanalyst

1

The Fascinating Subject Of Sex

Everyone wants to know *something* about sex. There is always *some* question you would like to have answered, no matter how old you are. A grandmother, for instance, knows a good deal about it but still wonders. Her daughter has told her that nowadays doctors say it is safe to have sex while the woman is pregnant. Can that really be true? A man of 70 is thinking of getting married to a lady of 67. He wonders if they would have sex, and if it would be pleasing for each of them.

But young people who are just getting to the age of wondering about themselves and sex have many, many questions, and usually they have trouble finding someone who will answer them.

The problem is that for most people sex is very, very personal. Even when they talk about

1

it they hold back the questions they most want to ask. This is true of almost everyone, and it is very natural.

At the age when their bodies are changing in amazing ways, and when they sense changes in their feelings and desires, young people become uneasy. And they are especially uneasy about what other people expect them to do.

That's when people want someone who is trustworthy. Even with understanding parents, good teachers of sex education, helpful counselors at a church or synagogue, one has some questions to ask of a person who is somewhat apart, who treats the question as coming from a grown-up, who has good information, and who will keep the conversation confidential. Where is that wonderful adviser?

Looking for that source of information, thousands of young people have written to Dr. Ruth Westheimer, the "Dr. Ruth" of radio and television.

Nobody can give thorough guidance about serious personal problems by mail, but Dr. Ruth answers the letters and gives such commonsense answers as can be given, always having the good of the letter writer in mind.

The questions these letter writers ask show what young people are wondering about. Following are some examples:

I have never had sex with a boy. Am I normal?

I am popular and good-looking and very

smooth-talking with girls, but I am afraid to have sex.

All my friends have bigger boobs than I have. Can I do something to make mine grow?

My penis seems to be small for a boy my age.

I love my boyfriend very much but he wants to have sex and I don't.

If I swallow semen will I get pregnant?

Some girls and I used to fool around together. Can a man tell I'm a lesbian if I have sex with him?

I go to a psychotherapist and she arouses me sexually. Would she ever have sex with me?

I am 17 and have never had a period. My boyfriend says I can't get pregnant until I do. Is this true?

I go with a girl who is two years older than I am. She wants me to have sex with her but I want to wait, although I love her very much. I know she thinks I am partly gay. This makes me wonder, too.

My girl friends tease me because I am a virgin and I wonder if I should do it.

I have a boyfriend who is bisexual. I am not in love with him but I think about having sex with him just to find out about it.

If I pull my penis out before I come, can the girl get pregnant?

If I don't have an orgasm can I get pregnant?

If we do it standing up will that keep me from getting pregnant?

I have heard that wearing a condom won't always prevent catching V.D.

If my boyfriend gets blue balls, will that harm him sexually?

My friend says that I've *got* to do it sometime. Is this really so?

Good questions! And we are going to answer them *now*, rather than send anyone to another part of the book!

It is perfectly normal not to have had sex with a boy. Especially at this girl's age, which was 15.

The boy who is afraid to have sex shouldn't push himself. For some, this means waiting until they get married. The right time to have sex is when you and your lover each feel ready for it—old enough, independent enough, self-reliant enough, and really wanting sexual closeness with each other.

We prefer to call boobs "breasts"—they deserve a serious and loving word. Anyway, don't try to make your breasts bigger; instead, work on making your mind bigger so it understands that all the different-looking breasts in the world are things to revere, all being beautiful to the knowing eye. Especially, stay away from surgical monkey business with your body—it is an outrage!

Your penis is large enough. The next time you have an erection, look in a full-length mirror. It's a lot bigger-looking when you see it that way. Penis size and breast size are two things people get silly about. They have little to do with the realities of sex.

If you love your boyfriend and don't want to start sex, tell him both of these things. Say that you know he wants to have sex, but if *he* loves *you,* he has to understand that you are not ready for it. Sex under pressure is bad sex.

If you swallow semen you will not get pregnant, unless you also get some semen in your vagina. The digestive and reproductive systems are not connected by any passageway.

Lots of kids fool around sexually, both homosexually and heterosexually, both gay and straight. Except that it is not either gay or straight, but just kids fooling around. The only way anyone can know that you have had this experience is if you tell him. It leaves no mark on your body or on your behavior.

People who go to psychotherapists often fall in love with them. It is very natural and the psychotherapist is not surprised by it. But it would be wrong for this professional person to have sex with you. A psychotherapist has a different kind of part to play in your life!

If you don't want to get pregnant, don't have intercourse without contraception. A simple rule, easy to remember.

If your girl friend is trying to force you to have sex and sets you to wondering if you may be homosexual because you don't want to have sex, you really are being shoved around, and you need a different kind of girl friend at your present stage. One who feels the way you do about sex right now.

Friends who tease you about being a virgin are the wrong friends. Find some others.

Don't have sex just to find out about it. To find out about sex, read books on the subject. Actually having sex, using your own body for experimentation, will teach you less than you might think. You are more likely to learn about serious heartbreak or other troubles than to learn about sex.

Withdrawing your penis before ejaculating is a very poor form of contraception. Your erect penis secretes semen filled with lively sperm cells before you ejaculate. Besides, you can't always tell when you will ejaculate.

You *can* get pregnant if sperm gets into your vagina. That is all that is needed. Whether or not you enjoy yourself has nothing to do with it.

Having sexual intercourse standing up may not be enjoyable, but you can certainly get pregnant that way.

A condom can be a barrier against transmitting gonorrhea to your partner, but other diseases such as syphilis can go from one person to the next from sores on the skin into cuts in the skin. Very tiny cuts you don't even know are there.

When a boy or man has a strong erection, and no ejaculation, he may get an aching in the testicles and they may change color for a while. But the condition goes away and no damage is done. A man telling his girl friend, "Give me sex or I'll be ruined!" is just blackmailing her.

You'll have sex, and good sex, when you *want* to and there is someone who wants to have sex with you. There is no "have to" about sex, although there *is* a lot of "want to."

All these questions addressed to Dr. Ruth show, if anyone really doubted it, that young people have lots of questions about sex. And nobody close at hand whom they feel they can ask. And the questions show that while modern young people may seem to know all about sex, there is still a lot of important information that *they* know they don't have.

Young people want to discuss sex with someone who will not make them feel indecent or dumb, so they talk mostly to their own age group about it. People of one's own age understand feelings best—that's how people feel at almost every age. But it is one thing to understand feelings and another to have good information.

People like to talk to their own age group about sex mostly to get support about their feelings. It is easier to admit a very strong personal interest to someone your own age, who may have the same strong interest. Your own age group understands your wanting to talk about it often and at length.

A young person needs a way to get sex information without always asking a grown-up, and the grown-up needs a reliable book to recommend to a young person. Suppose a boy and his father have a nice long talk one night, but the next night the boy has another question and the father is busy. Right then the boy could use a good book on the subject. And for that boy, and for all the young people like him—all these young people with all these questions—we want to offer a book that will answer as many questions as possible.

GOOD INFORMATION AND BAD

It isn't just that people start out with no information about sex. A very big problem, leading to unwanted pregnancy, sickness, unhappiness, and feeling bad about sex instead of knowing it for a happy and natural part of human life, is that we have all around us a lot of harmful and misleading information.

You see it on TV, at the movies, in books and magazines, and you hear it from your friends. That's why so many schools, libraries, churches, and synagogues try to put *reliable* information in the hands of young people. Chances are that *you* got *this* book from such a source. Or from your parents, who know they can't give you all the information you want exactly when you want and need it.

As long as you live you can go on adding, little by little, new material to your store of sexual knowledge. New scientific discoveries about human sexuality are being made all the time, and these findings are reported in responsible papers, magazines, and books. And even on radio and TV!

TALKING ABOUT SEX

People of all ages talk about sex, just as people of all ages take part in sex. (In fact, even baby boys and girls, who can't yet talk, have erections and lubrication and pleasant feelings in their genitals and like to touch themselves there.)

Talking about sex is a useful way to improve your understanding. But a person who is cautious learns to think, "I wonder if what he said is really true?" And makes a note to get to the library and look it up, or to ask someone who knows for sure.

It is a good thing to realize that a good friend may have gotten hold of some faulty information. It doesn't lessen a friend's value to be mistaken once in a while.

SEX AND BABIES

You may not be interested in babies just now, but think about them for a moment. You are never far from babies. Look at your thumb—formerly a baby's thumb, and probably sucked by a baby: you. We were all babies once. We all have mothers and fathers, grandparents, great-grandparents, going back into unrecorded time—and every person on that enormous family tree was a baby, and every person's existence began with a sexual act. This is well known, but worth thinking about because it helps us to realize that sex is in every single human life. Never think of it as something weird that you dreamed up by yourself!

Babies are usually started by two people having sex. The man puts his penis into the woman's vagina. Young children, when they first hear of this, very often think they are being told a silly story. Nevertheless, that is how the act of impregnation is usually done. Sperm from the man's penis goes into the woman's vagina and swims up into her uterus. One tiny sperm unites with an egg cell (or ovum) in her fallopian tube. The fertilized egg cell grows and develops, and just about nine months later a baby is born.

You may know all that, but many young people apparently don't know it because even though they don't want to have babies they do have them.

Sometimes a couple wants to have a baby but the usual way of getting pregnant doesn't work for them. Then the woman may be impregnated by artificial insemination: The man masturbates, his semen is kept alive in a container, and a doctor puts some of it way up into the woman's fallopian tube and a sperm cell unites with an egg cell. This is not romantic in the ordinary sense, but it may be a joyful thing to the woman who wants a baby and to the man who wants to share one with her.

But sex that starts babies very often is *not* romantic. Two people who are just fooling around with sex, with no love between them, can start a baby very easily.

If you are only trying out sex, without any desire to have a baby, the sperm cell will still try to unite with that egg cell. The two cells care nothing about what you want. They know nothing about love, romance, or your plans to go to college and get started in a career. They will unite if they can, no matter how inconvenient that may be for you.

You don't have to have a good time to start a baby. Neither the man nor the woman has to enjoy it very much. The sex act can be too rushed for enjoyment, or perhaps only one person really wanted it. The penis doesn't even have to go all the way into the vagina—just far enough to put the semen there.

Young people have asked Dr. Ruth, "What if I get semen on my finger and put that finger inside her vagina?"

Yes. That *could* make her pregnant.

THE OTHER PURPOSE OF SEX

Human sex is not just for making babies. It is a way of expressing love between two people, of uniting their lives very closely.

For some people, sex is more a pleasure for its own sake than an expression of love or a way of getting close to another person. This is a well-known fact—we are not making it up. So, if you are in love and thinking of having sex with someone, you may want to make sure that the person feels the same way about you, is capable of feeling that way.

Recently Dr. Ruth took a phone call from a woman college student on her Sunday-night radio program. The student said she had been dating a male student for a long time, and before they had sex together he was very attentive and gave her help, companionship, the feeling of being wanted. After sex started, he had time only for sex. No more phone calls stretching on and on, no more meals or movies or shows together. Dr. Ruth told the caller to say good-bye to the fellow and find one whose interest in her, as opposed to his interest in sex for itself, was likely to last longer.

People may have a number of loves before settling down with a long-term one. But the bitter disappointment of finding that you have misunderstood a person completely, and have been used, and dumped, is not for a young teenager to face. It is hard enough for a person who is older and more sure about life and the future.

THE KIND OF PEOPLE WHO MAKE LOVE AND BABIES

All kinds of people make love and have babies, not just the sort of people you see on a soap opera or in a movie. All around the world, people of every color, speaking languages you don't understand, are doing this same human thing. But for you it is good to think about the people who passed on to your parents and to you the life they shared.

Is there a family album at home? Ask to see it and look at those real people—parents, grandparents, great-grandparents. These are the people who gave you your face and hands and feet and bone structure—and the capacity to have a life and to share it with another person.

What they gave to you is the most valuable

gift—yourself. You can take care of the gift they gave you or neglect it, but taking care of it will be the wise way. The physical body should be fed and rested and exercised every day, and the best time to form the easy habits that make the best of your body is now, while you are young. It is so much easier to keep a good habit than to break a bad one and try to start another.

People are right to be interested in the way they look. Looking well and feeling fine go together—looking good goes with a bright eye, nice movements, a good voice, a mind that is awake and enjoying being awake. In the family album look for the confident-looking person. Imagine the cheering way that person could talk, walk, go through the day's work and fun.

Especially while you are young and developing you can avoid taking harmful things into your body—and avoid getting into the habits that are so hard to break. Cigarettes, alcohol, drugs, candy, and foods you may be allergic to can be kept out of your body. And now is the best time to learn to enjoy the good foods that give you strength, vigor, alertness, and clear eyes and skin—that feed the face and body and brain that came to you from those people in the family album.

FROM BABY TO CHILD TO ADULT

So, every human being's life begins with a sex act—either a basic, unromantic act or a joyful one between people who love each other. And the new individual has sexual experiences from the start. A newborn boy has erections. His penis gets hard. A newborn girl can have wetness in her vagina and pleasant sexual feelings. Let's take each kind of person, male and female, through the stages of sexual growth.

FROM BOY TO MAN

The baby boy is already equipped with his sexual organs. The penis and testicles are visible when he is changed or bathed. The penis is like a little finger. Urine comes out of it. Sometimes the infant's penis may become stiff and erect, giving a preview of another use for this organ later on in life. As he gains control of his movements, the male child instinctively fondles his genitals. From his expression it is plain that the experience is pleasant for him.

The baby boy is born with a small ring of skin that slides over the tip of his penis. Some people remove this foreskin for religious reasons—notably, the Jews and Moslems. Other people do it to make washing the penis very easy. Then there is no need to pull back the foreskin to wash under it. Removing the foreskin is called circumcision. The foreskin loosely covers the head of the uncircumsized penis except during an erection, when the foreskin is drawn back and the enlarged head of the penis emerges.

A boy can feel his testicles inside the scrotum, or bag of thin skin, which holds them below his penis. The testicles are very sensitive and easily hurt. When the boy reaches puberty, his sexual development includes the production of sperm in his testicles. The sperm is carried in a milky fluid called semen. During sexual intercourse, the semen is ejaculated through the erect penis into the woman's vagina, carrying millions of microscopic sperm. When just one of the sperm unites with one ovum, or egg cell, from one of the woman's ovaries, a baby is started.

Before puberty, the boy's penis may become erect, but his glands produce no seminal fluid, his testicles no sperm. At a certain point in puberty he begins to have ejaculations either through masturbating or involuntarily in his sleep.

At puberty his body begins to change in many ways. The testicles produce male hormones that enter the bloodstream and begin to bring about the changes. The boy grows taller, heavier, and his voice deepens. His penis and testicles grow larger, and hair starts to grow around these organs. Hair will also sprout under his arms and on his chest, and he may think it is time to shave his face.

Touching and playing with the penis is something babies and toddlers do, and they may go on doing so privately right up until puberty, or may stop it for a while. Most boys begin to masturbate at puberty, touching and stroking the penis until it is erect and until it ejaculates semen. Even today some people think

At puberty, the boy's body begins to change in many ways. He grows taller, heavier, and his voice deepens. The penis and testicles grow larger and hair starts to grow around these organs. Hair also begins to grow under his arms and on his chest.

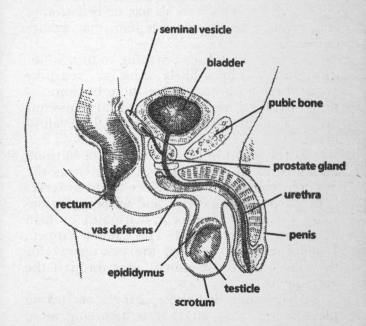

labels in figure:
seminal vesicle
bladder
pubic bone
prostate gland
urethra
penis
rectum
vas deferens
epididymus
testicle
scrotum

Male Reproductive Organs

Sperm cells are formed in the testes and stored in the epididymis, where they ripen. The sperm cells then travel through the tube called the *vas deferens* to another storage area located outside the testicles called the seminal vesicles.

that masturbation is immoral and harmful, but we know that nearly all men and boys masturbate, and no one can show that it has done them any harm.

The boy who does not masturbate, or who does it seldom, will have "wet dreams." These are also called "nocturnal emissions." While he sleeps, his penis becomes hard and semen spurts out, drying quickly on pajamas or bed clothes and leaving a stiff, yellowish stain that washes out easily.

No one should say anything to him about these stains as he is likely to be very sensitive about discussing his private thoughts and actions involving sex. The nocturnal emissions are a sign of health and normal development.

At this point in life the boy begins to think of his penis as a sexual organ as well as the organ he urinates through. Since the penis serves both purposes, some girls and women may develop a partial dislike for it, fearing that a man might urinate into them. This cannot happen. When the penis is erect, the passageway for urine is shut. Urine cannot pass through the erect penis.

At the time that these changes are taking place in the boy's body he is becoming more grown-up in many ways. He begins to take part in high-school sports, and to think about what kind of life he will lead as a man after his education is finished. What kind of work will he do? Often he has a hobby, such as auto repairing or electronics, that may turn into his life's work.

And he begins to have a new kind of interest in girls.

FROM GIRL TO WOMAN

The baby girl is born with her sexual organs in place, though they are small and inactive. Externally you can see only a little cleft below the baby's belly, between her legs. But inside her abdomen are two ovaries that already contain a complete store of microscopic eggs. Leading from each ovary are the tiny fallopian tubes, which enter the womb, or uterus. The womb is the place in the mature woman where the fertilized ovum will nest and grow until, in about nine months, the baby is ready to be born.

Leading from the uterus is the vagina, a small passageway to the outside of the body. The vagina is the organ that in a mature woman receives the penis during intercourse. And it is through the vagina that the newborn infant is gradually pushed until it reaches the outside world. In the infant and young girl, the vagina is extremely small. It is not ready for any insertions; trying to push anything into an infant's or child's vagina is extremely dangerous.

The girl's sexual parts that can be seen from the outside are called, all together, the vulva, and they too are important. Surrounding the opening to the vagina are two folds of skin called the inner lips. Some girls and women enjoy having these lightly touched or stroked.

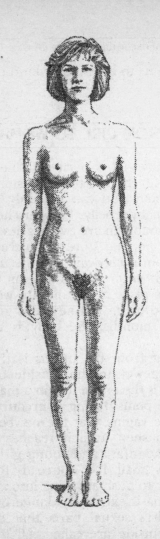

At puberty the girl's body begins to change in several obvious ways. Her slim, boyish legs and hips fill and round out. As her breasts enlarge, so do the nipples. Her voice deepens as she grows taller. Hair begins to grow under her arms, on her legs and around the genital area.

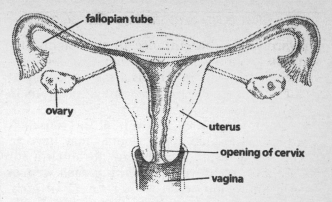

Frontal View of the Female Reproductive Organs

The girl's sexual organs that can be seen from the outside are called, all together, the vulva. Surrounding the vagina are the inner lips. Where the inner lips come together is the clitoris, a highly sensitive organ. At the top of the vagina is the cervix, which is the bottom portion of the uterus. The ovaries produce the female hormone, estrogen, which causes eggs to be released. The eggs then travel toward the uterus through the fallopian tubes.

Side View of the Female Reproductive Organs

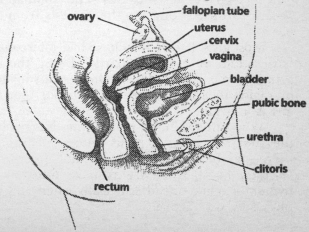

Upward from the entrance to the vagina, toward her belly, where the inner lips come together, is the clitoris. This is a soft, pea-shaped organ that is small, even in some adult women. It is very sensitive.

When the clitoris is touched, the sensation can be so enjoyable that a woman may have an orgasm as a result. Exactly how to touch it for the greatest pleasure is something each woman has to know and teach to her lover. In girls, the clitoris is covered by a little fold of skin that can be moved aside. When the genitals have been stimulated and are engorged, the clitoris expands and becomes erect like a little penis.

Glands in the vagina secrete a moisture that wets the walls of the vagina when the woman is sexually aroused. She may be aroused by an intimate scene in a book or movie, for instance. This is normal bodily functioning. Even very, very nice girls experience this. The command to become aroused comes to the genitals from the brain.

Most girls, before they have had intercourse, have a fold of thin skin partly closing the entrance to the vagina. This is the famous hymen, or maidenhead, supposedly the proof that the girl is a virgin.

When this skin, or membrane, is stretched the first few times a penis enters the vagina, there may be a little blood, but not necessarily. In fact, many true virgins have little or no hymen or maidenhead, especially when they are physically very active.

The girl's outlet for urine is in the genital area, between the inner lips and above the entrance to the vagina and below the clitoris. She has no tube to urinate through and cannot stand up and aim a stream of urine, so she usually sits or squats while urinating. In girls as in boys, urinating is a process distinct from sexual functioning.

As the girl grows from childhood to puberty her body begins to change in several obvious ways. Hormones are sent from the ovaries as signals for the changes to begin. Breasts develop. Slim, boyish legs and hips fill and round out. As the breasts enlarge, so do the nipples, which become more prominent. The girl's voice deepens somewhat as she grows taller; hair grows under her arms, on her legs, and over the pubic bone just above the genital area and around the vulva.

MENSTRUATION

These changes take place at different ages in different girls, causing some rivalry and anxiety both in those who change early and those whose bodies mature later. Most changes take place gradually, but the first menstruation is a distinct event, coming suddenly and definitely. It may happen anytime between the ages of 11 and 17, roughly.

Menstruation is the period in the cycle of female body processes when the ovaries release egg cells. First one ovary releases an egg; then, about twenty-eight days later, the other ovary releases one. The fallopian tube moves the egg cell along toward the uterus. Once in the uterus, if the egg cell has not been fertilized by a sperm cell, it is sent down through the vagina to be expelled from the body.

When the egg cell leaves the uterus it is carried along with the blood-rich lining of the uterus. When this lining, which has disintegrated into a fluid, seeps or rushes out of the vagina, it means that once again the lining is not needed to nourish a beginning baby.

Menstruation may look like bleeding, but it is not. There are no cuts or wounds inside the female. It is not like losing part of the vital blood supply, and there is not much menstrual fluid produced, even though sometimes it may *seem* like a lot.

Menstruation is a normal bodily process, not a sickness. Sometimes the muscles that push out the unneeded material cause some tension and cramps. For many girls, there is no reason to stay home or stop their usual activities, though some girls feel more comfortable if they take things easy during part of the menstrual period. It is not unusual for girls to feel better if they exercise. Each girl will find out what is best for her, but it is definitely not a time to stay in bed or load up with painkillers. If the girl finds menstruation a difficult time, she should have a talk with her doctor or school nurse.

A PRIVATE BUSINESS

There is no need to tell parents or friends that the menstrual period has returned, though girls do commonly mention the fact in passing to girl friends or to their mothers. Following advice from her mother, school nurse, or doctor, the girl will use a tampon or sanitary napkin to absorb the menstrual fluid. A virgin can use a tampon, which may not disturb the hymen at all or may stretch it just a little. Using the tampon or sanitary napkin and keeping her body clean are the girl's own responsibility.

Many girls find the menstrual period a very minor business that becomes more important when they become sexually active, with intercourse, and either want to get pregnant or do not. When pregnancy has begun, menstruation stops! Sexually active girls and women watch for that as a sign of pregnancy.

This is why girls and women watch the calendar to see if the menstrual period comes on the expected day or shortly after it. If menstruation is delayed, a doctor should be consulted; it may mean there is a pregnancy or some medical problem, and the girl should know.

INTERCOURSE AND BABIES

A loving couple, feeling tender and warm with each other, wanting to hold and caress and touch, are acting in a sexual way. All these feelings and actions move the couple toward sexual intercourse. The man's erection at such intimate moments is preparation for intercourse, and so is the woman's lubrication and the increased openness of her genitals. When the man's penis enters the vagina, it drips a small amount of semen containing thousands of sperm. This happens even before ejaculation. These sperm immediately move toward the ovum to fertilize it. And it takes only one sperm to unite with the ovum for pregnancy to begin.

With the movements of intercourse come the pleasures of it, and on ejaculation millions of sperm are sent on their way to find the ovum, which may or may not be waiting and ready, depending on the time in the menstrual cycle. All the unused sperm, which are contained in a small amount of seminal fluid, are absorbed harmlessly into the female's body.

When the egg cell, or ovum, is in the fallopian tube, waiting to come down into the womb, or uterus, and one sperm finds it, they unite. Male and female are now truly one in that newly fertilized ovum. It moves downward, finds and attaches to a place in the lining of the uterus, and the embryo begins to develop.

THE MOTHER AND THE BABY'S GROWTH

This embryo, microscopic in size, is the new baby, growing inside its mother. It is attached in the uterus by a cord, really a tube, that brings nourishment from the mother's body to the baby. During the next nine months the mother is responsible for the baby's development. She can affect the baby by what she eats, what she drinks, what drugs she takes, and whether she smokes.

The woman's responsibilities for the baby's life are great, and they are just starting. And of course the husband and father who stays, helps his wife and takes responsibility for his child, makes a large contribution. When the couple are happy they have a sense that the baby is *theirs*, and that it is now the center of their lives.

As the baby grows, the mother's abdomen becomes rounder and bigger. Her breasts grow larger, and her nipples, with the area around them, become larger, ready to feed the baby after it is born.

Breasts, especially in the United States and Europe, and in countries populated by people who come from Europe, are admired and desired. This feeling for them, and the part they play in lovemaking, makes us forget sometimes that their basic purpose is to supply babies with the best nutrition they can be given—mother's good milk.

At the end of about nine months the baby is fully formed. It is able to breathe air, to suck, to see, and to continue to grow. It is ready to be born! The baby comes from the uterus into the vagina and out into the great world.

THE EXPERIENCE OF GIVING BIRTH

It is the woman who carries the baby inside her body, and she is the one who gives birth to it. It is each woman's own experience, and only she knows just how she feels about it. While a birth is usually a very exciting event for both parents, even for very well-informed ones, it can be looked forward to and experienced calmly if both mother and father are well prepared for it. The mother needs good care and advice from a doctor before the birth. It is very helpful if both parents go to classes that prepare them for the part each is to play during pregnancy and birth and in caring for the baby afterward.

Many women give birth rather easily. Those who have more difficulty can limit their own fear and pain by trusting good doctors and nurses and by fully cooperating with them. There are risks to both mother and child, but most births are normal, and when both parents care for and support each other, and look forward happily to having their child, birth is a wonderful thing to share.

READY OR NOT?

The boy who can ejaculate semen may be only in junior high school, but he is capable of impregnating a girl or woman. The girl who is ovulating—that is, whose ovaries release egg cells into her fallopian tubes—may not be ready for adult life, but if semen gets into her vagina she can become pregnant. And either the boy or the girl may be having strong urges to get close physically to some attractive person.

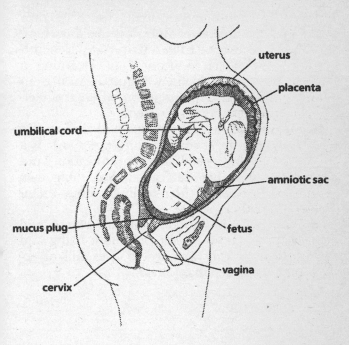

uterus

placenta

umbilical cord

amniotic sac

fetus

mucus plug

vagina

cervix

Pregnancy

During the first weeks of pregnancy, the embryo develops from a single cell into a recognizable human being. In the uterus, the embryo is cushioned by the uterine wall and wrapped in a fluid-filled amniotic sac, which is surrounded by the placenta. From the twelfth week on, the embryo is called a fetus. It receives oxygen and nourishment from its mother through the umbilical cord.

Both of them have to learn a great deal before they can be, and feel themselves to be, ready to take full responsibility for their own lives. That complete readiness may be anywhere from six to twelve or fifteen years away, depending on how much education and training a chosen life and work may require. And, even more important, depending on when the feeling of readiness comes to them.

Meanwhile, sexual feelings and desires are powerful in a great many young people. It is a time when they need all the education and understanding they can get about their own sexuality and about their feelings about themselves and other people.

This book is for you who are young and who want to know all you can about living and loving and looking forward to lives full of accomplishment and happiness.

2

Is There Love Without Sex?

We hear a lot of young people telling how they feel about love and sex. We mean young people from about 11 to about 18, but this age group says many of the same things and asks many of the same questions as older people do.

Is there love without sex? Sex without love? Aren't they really two different things? Or are they really different parts of the same thing? These questions become serious for people of every age.

Different people feel differently about these questions and give different answers. Furthermore, each person feels differently about love and sex at different times in his life. A very young person finding out about life, and all the things that are to be done in it, certainly feels different from an older person who has or

31

who wants some one person with whom to share life, and wants a strong bond with that person.

Each of the following statements represents a certain way of feeling about love and sex at a certain time in life.

A girl says, "I couldn't 'do it' with a boy I didn't love."

Another one says, "But I fall in love with a new guy every week! Maybe it's just sex and I only think it's love."

Here is a boy: "I guess I love my mom and dad. And my grandma. Sometimes I love her most. When I look at girls or think about them I think about their bodies and sex. I know what they mean about love, but I have to admit I don't really feel that."

"When I make out with someone, it's physical. I don't want to talk about love. I might pretend it's love because they want me to, but really I want to fool around. And I think about going the whole way all the time."

"I guess I fall in love with girls. I don't really date them much. Once or twice is all, so far, really. I'm embarrassed to tell a girl how I feel, and especially to say what I really want to do. I daydream about sex with different girls, but I always think about being in love with them *and* having sex. I really love their hair and eyes and faces and bodies, and would love to have a girl and be her boyfriend. But when I was touching her or having sex with her it would really be for me, and I wouldn't tell her that. I'd let her think it was love, though."

"I've been friends with her since we were 10. That was four years ago. I guess we might even get married. We like each other—anyway, we seem to. And I'm not afraid of her. She doesn't giggle and act like I'm weird because I'm a boy. She is nice but not sexy. I guess I don't think about her when I think about sex. She is too nice. And not sexy."

"I fall in love with girls a lot. I really go crazy about them. I can't think of anyone else for a while. But then sometimes I have sex or fool around with one and the love goes away."

"Right now I am in love with three different girls. Two in school and one on my block who goes to another school. I think sexy thoughts about them and about a lot of 'Tens' in the movies and TV. I never really dated any of these girls. I guess I don't really want a girl friend."

"A lot of guys say love is just a joke but they want lots of sex. But I have had sex with girls, and when I am having sex I feel like I love them. But it goes away until the next time I have sex."

"I love him. We have been in love for two years. I love having sex with him, but if we couldn't have sex I would still love him."

"I have been going with her a long time and we don't go with anyone else. But I think we are both afraid to have sex and we both think we will marry someone else later on."

"I am in love with a really beautiful girl but

she won't even talk to me. I have some friends who are girls and we get along fine. Sometimes we have fights and make up, just like friends. Sometimes I'll be with one of these friends and things will get sexy. But it isn't like being in love."

That's enough to show how very different different people feel, and how much confusion there is about love and sex in people's lives.

Most people have the idea of being in love someday with a sexual partner and staying with that person. *Someday.* Almost everybody has that idea about the future, even if he or she can't put sex and love together right now.

WHEN THINGS GET SEXY

It happens so often to people that they *like* each other but just don't want to say yet that they are ready to be seriously in love. Opportunities for friendship come quite often. And opportunities for getting sexy come without any mention of love.

How should a young person act when that happens? *Stupid?* Or should one go along with it and see what happens? You can feel stupid backing away when you don't even know whether it's just friendly boy-girl stuff or getting serious. Or whether both of you really want to get sexy without making a real commitment.

Boys and girls in school, in clubs, in their usual ways of being together, have the chance to learn about one another. In the first place, they see appearances. Who's pretty, who's handsome, who dresses in the latest style, who is funny and fun to hang out with, who's boring, who thinks he or she is the absolute best, and who tries to beat everybody out at everything.

Boys and girls who like each other and go places together often touch. They might kiss hello or good-night. That seems to be the way to act. But a little signal like that has to be understood on both sides! Sometimes there has to be a friendly talk to make it clear that a friendly touch or kiss is not an "I love you" or a promise of sex.

A boy, being more easily aroused than most girls, may sometimes get the idea that a girl is interested in having sex with him when in fact she isn't. All she wants is to be friendly. And they hold hands or dance or pair up for games or going home. But then to her surprise he "tries something." How did he get *that* idea?

The way it happens is often something like this. One day the boy and girl are alone by chance and one takes the other's hand. Just a friendly thing, or a signal? They laugh and kid and kiss; he touches her leg, then higher. She laughs and clamps her thighs together. He laughs. She says, "Maybe we'd better find the others."

She partly liked what he was doing, but enough was enough. So she stopped him in a friendly way, and he laughed and they got up and went to find the others.

But she doesn't know that his penis got

hard and a little oozy, or that he was embarrassed because the erection did not go down right away.

Another time, these friends go a little further, and she doesn't seem to mind when he puts his hand over her breast. And when he slips his hand under her top and feels her nipple, it gets hard. Then she senses that he is going to try for "home base" again, sliding a hand up her leg, and she sits up and says, "Mmmm—what a beautiful day. Let's go do something." She means something else!

She realizes that she was getting a little oozy, but she doesn't have any idea of the condition he is in, or that he might be mad at her. All she did was change the subject in a friendly way, right?

But this time he doesn't laugh, because his penis is very hard and when his erection goes down his testicles will ache. Her cheerful, friendly manner right now seems definitely malicious, because she let him go that far, let him get really "hot," and then cut him off.

Didn't she let him touch her nipples? Didn't her nipples get hard? So she wanted it, too—but it was more fun to run off, leaving him aching.

She knows he's angry but she doesn't really know why. He thinks she has been teasing him on purpose. How does this happen?

Some girls are more slowly aroused than boys. Very often the girl thinks that what they are doing is interesting, a little scary but fun. And she has some interesting feelings. But she doesn't want to go too far, and she isn't so carried away that she forgets this. And she doesn't realize that a boy is likely to be much more aroused by a little petting than she is.

It is a perfect misunderstanding between friends. Neither of these two understands the other's ideas and feelings at all.

We would like to think that a week later one of them will hand the other a copy of this book and say, "Read chapter two." Because there is no reason that they can't be good friends.

Sometimes it's the girl who wants to fool around and the boy who is more cautious. The boy likes to kiss girls even if he isn't in love, but he doesn't want more. They touch a little, but she is bolder than he is. He is terribly embarrassed because he thinks it isn't manly to be the one who backs out, but even so, he does. Her feelings are hurt. It happens!

He can call her up later and say, "I hope you're not mad at me."

"I'm mad at you."

"Don't be mad at me. It's bad enough that you think I'm a homosexual."

"I don't think that. I think I'm humiliated."

"I'll meet you at the Friendly and buy you a Fribble."

"No."

"Cheeseburger."

"No."

"Oh, come on."

"Okay."

WHEN VERY YOUNG PEOPLE GET INTO SEX

If you follow the news, you know that lots of very young people are having sexual intercourse. Some of them come out of it pretty well and go on with their lives. But too many have trouble that is really too much for very young people. Pregnancy, having babies that have to be given away, having abortions, having V.D. Going through an agony of emotions. Causing distress for people all around them.

It is true that very young people can fall in love with an intensity that can be heart-wrenching. The story of Romeo and Juliet, put on the stage almost four hundred years ago, is the great love story of all time. But *Romeo and Juliet* is a tragedy.

Young people who are able to fall in love and have sex are, unfortunately, too young to support themselves and the babies they may have.

In the time of Romeo and Juliet, very young people did marry if their families agreed. But in those days the families did not expect a couple to set up a separate home and earn their own way. Today a couple must be older, better educated, and trained to make a living and to behave responsibly on their own, before they can begin a lifetime commitment.

LOVE OR SEX?

Do young people just old enough to have sex physically really want love, or is it just sex they want?

Boys are apt to say that when they are ready it could be any girl. Any girl who is ready and willing. But girls are not likely to become ready and willing unless they are to some extent in love with the boy.

A boy may find that there is a girl who is willing to pet and neck without fussing about love. This is often a girl who makes out or has sex with a number of boys. An emotional problem for some of the boys she makes out with is that they like the contact with a girl but want something more, a personal liking, a feeling that she has some special regard for the one she is with. This is usually out of the picture because making out and having sex are a kind of barter system for her. She uses them to keep herself in company, rides, ice cream, shows, and so on. Another problem with the girl who has a lot of close contacts with boys is that she can catch herpes, gonorrhea, or another STD (sexually transmitted disease) and pass it on to *all* her boyfriends. No fun for her, of course, but no fun for the guys, either.

On the other hand, the girl you really like and who seems to really like you may be a no-sex girl. Perhaps after you go with her awhile she will want you to hold her and kiss her. A friendship of this sort has many things going for it. You have a companion, a friend, the sense of being liked. No fear of pregnancy or infection.

There are many young people who love each other for being what they are—good friends, caring, thoughtful, considerate, fun to be with. And there are usually common interests— places to visit, people to be with, games and sports, music, shows, a whole expanding social life.

Many very young couples agree that sex is for the future, for sometime when it seems right for both of them.

SEX DOESN'T MAKE LOVE STAY

It's great for a young person to have a regular date who is a friend, who talks everything over with you, gives and takes advice, shares ups and downs with you. This is good for boys and girls.

Teenage loves are not necessarily going to last forever. But why spoil a lovely thing with depressing predictions? While people are in love it seems "forever."

"Our love was forever. No one else could ever be the one for me. She felt the same."

"How long did it last?"

"Two years."

"Pretty good!"

Breaking up a love causes heartache; but nearly everyone has survived it at some time. It is better, when the breakup comes, if neither you nor your lover has put too much into it, if neither one feels used and abandoned.

There is a point in many loves when the girl thinks, "If I don't let him have sex he'll go where he can get it, and I'll lose him." What follows after she thinks this may be the makings of a song or six months of a soap opera, of course. But people who are desperately trying to hang on to a lover should know this: sex doesn't make love last.

Lovers may go on loving for a long time—with or without sex. They may decide to marry after a long time together—with or without sex. But having sex doesn't keep a lover who seems likely to leave. Trying to hang on to someone is the wrong reason for starting a sexual relationship.

Love affairs without strong elements of companionship, mutual support, and caring are very likely to become stale and routine—and sex does not make up for everything that is missing. Sex is not the thing that keeps people together. It is more likely to be the other way around—people who suit each other well are apt to have good sex together! The divorce courts are crowded with cases in which sex did not save the marriage.

IF YOU REALLY LOVED ME

"If you really loved me you would go to bed with me," the fellow says to the girl. It is more often the male who uses this line, because the male is more easily aroused.

This male may really be a nice guy, but when he says this he is, temporarily, a blackmailer. He knows she is attached to him, likes the social life he provides, has given up other guys to be his girl, and is afraid of losing him. He isn't a real heel, trying to use this leverage to get her to have sex, because he thinks it would be nice for both of them. But he has lost sight of the fact that she has her own point of view. He is really forcing her to go against her feelings.

She may give in to him. But she wonders, "Will he always treat me like this, when it's what he wants against what I want?" And she thinks, "Is this what he is really like?"

BUT WHAT IF YOU ARE REALLY IN LOVE?

You may both really be in love, when your lover, whether you are the male or the female member of this love, wants to begin having sex. It is not always the male who makes the first moves toward greater intimacy. So, what now?

You may feel that sex would be a part of the love between you and your lover, that you want it too. And if you are sure that you are both strong enough, self-reliant enough, responsible enough to deal with the possible consequences of having sex, the decision is yours to make.

In our opinion, however, no young teenager is ready to make that decision. At that age, warmth and friendship, some kissing, and perhaps some harmless petting are the right expressions of love and happiness.

Some teenager will read this and say, "This doesn't apply to me and my lover. Our love is real and will last forever." It may be a girl who says that.

Blessings on you, young lover, and on your beloved! But consider this: sex put off as something for the future, as part of the dream you and your love share, can be a very binding thing. Many schoolday loves have lasted into marriage and on into the sunset of life. But full-scale sexual relationships begun too early have a way of peaking soon and then dying a pretty boring death.

3

It's Your Choice

This chapter is about things you can do sexually.

What you do sexually is *your* business! The choices are yours to make.

Your parents probably have warned you of things to avoid, and they did so to protect you. When we say it's your choice, we aren't questioning the right of your parents to teach and guide—not at all. But young people should be protected with knowledge. They have to know what things they can safely say yes to and when good sense determines that they say no.

What if Mom and Dad are very strict, what if they say no sex, no petting, no kissing, no hand-holding, stay away from it all? It is not our business to correct them. All caring parents want to set some limits, if only for the safety and survival of their children. But most parents do set reasonably lenient limits for their children. They don't want them to grow up in a prison and then to be turned loose in a world they don't know how to deal with at age 18 or so.

Controls are absolutely necessary for all of us, at any age, and especially as we learn to take part in life. We learn not to dash out into the street in front of cars; later we learn to drive safely and to deal wisely with invitations to drink, take drugs, and have sex. To act wisely, you need controls, but the controls must be in your *own* mind, because *you* are the one who will be getting the invitations. You are the one who decides whether to say yes or no.

If a boy says, "Let's do it," and the girl says, "No, I don't want to," she is the one who refuses. Not her mother.

If a boy feels like having sex but thinks the girl may have V.D., and then he decides to risk V.D. because he wants to have sex that badly—who makes the final decision? Not his parents. They are not feeling that strong urge. They warned him against this very thing. The control, or lack of it, is in the boy's mind.

The best preparation for dealing with sexual opportunities is to know as much as possible about sex—the pleasures to be expected, the limitations of the pleasures, and the dangers.

We don't want anyone to be scared to death of sex. In this we agree with most parents, who want their children to have a good life ahead with all of life's richness and pleasure. Sex is part of love and marriage. Young people should come to it hopefully, happily. They should know as much as possible about sex before experiencing its fullest pleasures, so that their choices are real choices and not bets in a game of chance.

In considering the choices possible in sexual behavior, let us start with what is available to the virgin, who would seem to have all the choices still ahead of her. Or *him*.

VIRGINS TODAY

Today, many brides are virgins, either because they are expected to be virgins or because they want to be. You may have heard otherwise, but this is the truth.

How can you be sure a girl is a virgin? This question used to worry people more than it does now, and even now Dr. Ruth is asked by men how to tell for sure. The answer is, "Don't make a fuss about whether a girl has never had *any* sexual experience; instead, think more about whether she is loving and lovable, a good companion, a cheering and admirable girl or woman." Strictly speaking, only the girl can be sure that she has never had sex with a male.

It used to be said that a virgin always had a hymen, that ring of membrane around the entrance to the vagina. If the bridegroom did not have to stretch the hymen on the wedding night, if there was no blood on the sheet, he had been cheated! This caused a lot of needless anxiety when completely inexperienced brides just didn't bleed. And many of them did not.

Nowadays, a girl or woman is considered a virgin until she has had intercourse with a man, and whether she is one or not is pretty much her business. When women, or men, really are virgins, this is of more importance to themselves than to anyone else. Among young teenagers and even older ones, choosing to remain a virgin offers some very practical advantages.

By waiting until she meets a man she can trust to be kind and considerate, the virgin avoids a rough introduction to sexual intercourse. The ordeal of first intercourse is probably exaggerated in many people's minds, but that first time can be unpleasant if it is with a selfish or clumsy male. The girl who wants a gentle and loving introduction to sex is wise to remain a virgin until the right man comes her way.

The well-informed female virgin knows that the early experiences of sex are usually imperfect, and that sex gets better as one becomes used to it with a certain partner. The good sex between them is something they create together, with growing understanding of each other and of sex. Since rough-and-tumble sex such as people have before they find a serious, committed lover is not the *best*, the virgin believes that her best plan is to live without sex until the time is right and the man is right.

In addition, the virgin often feels that she

wants to grow and develop within herself, to realize her own full growth *as* herself, before becoming so intimately involved with someone who may influence her strongly. She does not want to be so strongly influenced, to let another person come into her physically and mentally, before she really knows for certain who and what she is.

The time at which virgins feel ready to take part in sex is not determined by age measured in years, but simply in the development of strong self-confidence. Some people are very mature and self-confident at 18; some develop more slowly.

There may be in the female virgin a wish to be fully grown before she begins to risk giving her body and mind over to bearing children and caring for them.

And we must not forget the female resentment of male domination. That feeling is strong in many a virgin. She may be willing to let a man come into her life in time, when she is ready, and when he shows that his attitude toward her is right. Meanwhile, no man is going to have sex with her just because he hands her a bouquet or buys her a meal.

These reasons to stay a virgin for a while spring from personality and emotions. But there are also hardheaded reasons—and these are good reasons for girls and for boys as well.

The young male in the seventh to the twelfth grades will find that being active sexually with girls is a terrific strain. The anxieties of it are something he doesn't need. He doesn't need to be deceiving his parents, worrying about seeming ridiculous in the girl's eyes, worrying about pregnancy and herpes and the other forms of V.D.

Frequently he is driven back into staying a virgin not so much by these fears but because he is too busy to get into heavy sex. He has his science-fair projects, his computer mania, his record collection, his sports. These are so overwhelmingly interesting to him that all the sex he has time for is occasional masturbation, or perhaps a "wet" dream.

The girl who has her own strong interests in studies or activities, who is sometimes so misunderstood that people wish she could let up and "have a good time," is also willing to put off sexual involvement until later on, when she has time to spare from all her other interests.

It would be unrealistic not to mention the virgins who are choosing this path not out of fear, or because they are too preoccupied, but because of their religious upbringing. There are still young men and women who are taught to remain virgins until they marry—which they often do at a fairly early age. It is not as hard a life that these young people lead as out-siders might think. They have the support and approval of family, of friends, and of their faith. As abstaining from sex is only one of the disciplines in their lives, they have much more practice in self-control than most youngsters. These disciplines are more helpful than pain-ful. Daily prayers, religious observances, church or synagogue attendance, meditation, all give an order to life that is very comforting. Living by rules is, for most people, more comfortable than living by impulse. This is very useful to know, especially for those of us who are forced to make our own rules, or to choose them for ourselves.

The virgin girl can be a good friend to sexually active girls, listening to their troubles sympathetically. Often she knows more about periods, pregnancy, and steps to take when one is in trouble than does the sexually active girl. The virgin has the time to read up on things. And her cooler judgment often makes her the adviser to others.

TECHNICAL VIRGINS

A technical virgin is not a virgin working in a high-technology field, but just a very shrewd person who enjoys a bit of sexual activity but doesn't think it worthwhile to risk pregnancy. Her contraceptive method works one hundred percent. To sum it up, her method can be called *Anything Goes Except Going All the Way.* She may let her boyfriend fondle her or masturbate her, and she may do the same for him, but she always has her wits about her and refuses to have intercourse.

We do not urge anyone to choose this technical virginity without giving it some thought. It really isn't for everybody. Sometimes, and in some circles, the tech virgin is not regarded with great respect, even now, and that can make her feel a little cheap until her high spirits return. Some youngsters—a lot of youngsters, in fact—are not self-confident and assertive enough to carry off this policy. Tech virgins get a bad case of the blues now and then. But they are *never* as blue as someone who is in the tenth grade and pregnant.

Boys can be tech virgins, too. Obviously, they have forms of sex that do not include inserting their penises into vaginas. When teased about being "chicken" to go the whole way, they can brave it out by wearing a Zero Population Growth button.

Tech virgins learn a good deal about sexual technique that they can use all their lives when giving and receiving pleasure. But we must add that those techniques can be learned at any age, and there is no reason to learn them very early.

Frequently a couple who go around together for a long time, planning to marry, will practice tech virginity together. And they do marry, and often recall their old cautious pleasures very sentimentally.

TEENAGE FORMER VIRGINS

Often Dr. Ruth talks to or counsels young people who have been having sex with one or more partners. If they are *very* young, she urges them to drop out of the sexual rat race for a few years and concentrate on growing up. And, whatever age they are, she urges them to use contraception.

These young people are not all desperately unhappy—not by any means. There is a wide personality range among teenagers who are sexually active. If a young person asks what to do when urged into certain sex acts, there is always the same answer: don't give in to pressure. Avoid the person who tries to use pressure. Sometimes a girl is involved with an older, married man; the advice is to get out of that relationship, because the girl is being used. Married men almost never leave their wives for the teenage girls they have been using.

Frequently young people ask Dr. Ruth a question about a love affair that is going sour. When told to get out of it, they say that they had all but decided to do just that. They call the radio or TV program for support and encouragement to do so.

Whatever young people ask about sex, contraception, jealousy, normalcy, or emotional problems in a love affair, Dr. Ruth answers cheerfully and easily. Now and then she scolds people for doing something very stupid and self-destructive, but there is no disapproval for asking a question of any kind. In all this Dr. Ruth tries to be the friendly, reliable, respectful adviser so many youngsters are looking for.

Here is something that young people often find hard to do. Once they have begun to have sex, they find it hard to retrace their steps. This is especially true for girls. Naturally, Dr. Ruth encourages these young people to follow their instincts and get back into being kids and out of being used. It is interesting that these young people, usually girls, do want to stop sex for a few years, until they understand themselves better and are in charge of their own lives.

The decision to have sex, either for a man or woman, is a personal one. Today, having sex before marriage is very widely accepted. But the decision is best made by a person who is established in a career, who has either the income to be independent or the sense of security that comes of being in some sound professional training program.

But, for the very young who are having sex, the most important thing is to be assured that they are still valuable human beings. Worth listening to, worth advising, worth encouraging to get on with their lives and to look forward optimistically.

THE 1,001 WAYS OF SEX

Where is that fabulous sex book that instructs one in the wild variety of ways to make love? Parisian ways, Persian ways, Arab, Indian, Chinese, Japanese?

Not to be discouraging, but there really are not 1,001 ways to "do it." There are a few ways, and there are a few variations on these few basic ways. But sex is not going out of style because there are just a few basic ways of doing it!

These have to be learned, however. The sex urge is inborn, but knowing how to have intercourse has to be taught. In the movie *The Blue Lagoon* a boy and girl grow up all alone on an island. They find out about love and sex without any instruction. It is amusing to think about what might really happen in such a case. The boy and girl would certainly find many ways of touching before they figured out how to have intercourse. Maybe they would *never* figure that out!

Most sex manuals describe the ways in which a woman can receive the penis into her vagina. There are not many ways. The first is the man-on-top position. The woman lies on her back, with the man above her. He supports his weight partly on his elbows. They are facing each other, and the man inserts his erect penis into her lubricated vagina. They remain in this position, moving as it pleases them to move, not separating their sexual organs until one or both of them has had an orgasm. This is called the "missionary position" because missionaries are said to have told their converts that this was the only permissible way.

FOREPLAY

The couple will usually engage in foreplay before insertion of the penis. Foreplay means hugging and kissing. Touching and kissing and sucking breasts and nipples. Stroking the woman's clitoral area. The man's erection is quickly achieved. The woman's lubrication may take longer and should always take place before the penis is inserted, and insertion should take place at her invitation, when she is ready.

FEMALE SUPERIOR

Many men and women like to reverse the man-on-top position. The man lies on his back with the woman above him. The woman inserts the penis into her vagina and adjusts herself until they are both comfortable. With the woman above, sitting and straddling him, she can control her movements very well. She can support herself with her arms, leaning forward but not lying on the man. This lets him touch her and stimulate her as he wishes with his hands. She can also lie forward on the man. Or, sitting astraddle, face the other way, toward his feet.

TURNING HER BACK ON HIM

The woman can turn her back as they both lie on their sides. She positions her body so that he can enter her vagina from the rear. This allows the man to insert his penis and to reach her clitoris with his hand to stimulate it; also to fondle her breasts, belly, and thighs. She can reach back and gently touch his testicles.

The selection of these various positions can be signaled by one or the other of the partners or discussed beforehand. Generally, a couple will have a favorite position and use that most of the time, switching to one of the others as their desires dictate.

SITTING POSITION

This is done on a chair or stool. The woman sits on the man's lap, facing him and straddling his thighs. Or she can face the other way. This is a restful position, good for gentle, friendly sex.

STANDING UP

This position is much favored for "quickie" sex. Since the woman has to spread her legs, it is best if she is as tall as the man or taller, or he will have to keep his knees half-bent throughout the performance. Sometimes the woman is lifted right off the floor, and wraps her legs around the man. Some women find this pleasing, but it can be very tiring for the man, and it allows small chance for touching with the hands in various places.

SIDEWAYS, FACE TO FACE

Lying on their sides and facing each other, the man and woman can have intercourse with one of the woman's legs under his and one over. And the leg arrangement can be varied experimentally.

COMING TO ORGASM

The man thrusts into the vagina at varying rates of speed until he has an orgasm and ejaculation. If the woman usually has an orgasm from intercourse, the man may want to delay his orgasm until after hers. Many couples use other techniques to bring the woman to orgasm. The man may fondle her clitoris while they are having intercourse, or she may fondle it; or he may stimulate her clitoris after intercourse has concluded, until she has had her orgasm. Or he may lick her clitoris with his tongue. This kind of stimulation of the clitoris is best taught to the man by the woman, so that he can do it just to her liking.

SEX WITHOUT INTERCOURSE

People enjoy many forms of sex play that don't involve intercourse, or putting the penis into the vagina. All these ways may be used by the technical virgin, mentioned earlier.

Masturbation, useful for solitary sex, is nice with a partner. The couple can masturbate each other, learning from each other the best ways to touch and stroke the penis and the clitoris. A tissue can be kept nearby to catch the man's ejaculation when it comes. Often the woman holds the man's testicles gently while masturbating him.

The couple can "do" each other at the same time or take turns. Many people prefer taking turns, each partner making a long work of art of "serving" the loved one. The masturbation should not be a race to reach orgasm, but slow and teasing to give the most exquisite pleasure.

FELLATIO AND CUNNILINGUS

Stimulating the penis to orgasm using lips and tongue is called fellatio. Cunnilingus is kissing, licking, and sucking the sensitive areas of the female genitals, either to arouse the woman before intercourse or to bring her to orgasm.

The woman learning fellatio is urged to think of an ice-cream cone. As she licks and sucks around the head of the penis, slowly, appreciatively, she is to think of a cone of her favorite flavor of ice cream. This is not to take her mind off what she is doing but rather to give her an idea of the best slow and teasing style.

Some women don't want to perform fellatio, and therefore they should never do so. There is nothing wrong with it, but some women do not like it. Doing it would build up resentment against sex with the man demanding it. And the man should not demand or pressure the woman about this.

Sometimes a woman changes her mind about fellatio. Often this is done on the spur of the moment, when the pressure to do it is off.

Should she swallow the semen? Or even take it in her mouth? Only if she wants to. It is quite harmless, but only if the boy has no venereal disease, of course. If she doesn't want to, she can ask him to say when he is about to come and catch the semen in a tissue.

Swallowing semen will not make her pregnant.

The male lover often wants to kiss and lick the woman's genitals, which can be very pleasurable to her. She can teach her lover the best way for her. Some women are a little displeased by this kind of play because they are afraid it will be unpleasant for the man. This is because they think of "down there" as being unclean. In fact, the female genitals clean themselves very nicely. Douching, or cleaning the vagina with water or various mixtures, used to be considered necessary, but now women are advised just to wash the outside genitals while showering.

The vagina has a fresh, pleasant odor all its own. If there is a stronger, less likable odor, there may be some kind of infection and the woman should get a visit her doctor to help clear it up.

Before lovemaking, and especially before licking and kissing the sexual parts, it is good fun and foreplay as well as good hygiene for the couple to shower together. But playing games in the shower should be careful and gentle to avoid accidents.

GIRLS MASTURBATE, TOO

Not all of them. And certainly not as many women masturbate as men do. But there are women who grow up fondling and stroking the clitoral area. There is no harm in doing this and none in not doing it.

Women are brought to orgasm less quickly than men, for the most part, and many women have actually never had an orgasm. In recent years the practice of masturbation has become more acceptable as private behavior, and many women have taught themselves to masturbate and through this to have orgasms. What they learn by themselves they can later teach to a lover. The woman places his hand where she wants it, telling him what she wants him to do and guiding his hand with her own.

MASSAGE

Massage has many uses. Athletes are given massage to relieve aches and strains in their muscles. Massage relieves muscular tension and brings circulation to the surface of the body. Massage can relax a tired person and bring sleep; it can be used to refresh a tired person for a big evening after a hard day.

Between lovers massage can be used both for comfort and for sexual arousal. Many people find massage very arousing, and when there is plenty of time for it there is no finer sort of foreplay. There are many good books on how to give massage, and anyone can learn the art well enough to do it.

Either the less tired partner massages the wearier one to restore vigor and a taste for pleasure, and then the couple proceed to genital play of some sort, or the two partners take turns giving massage to each other. It is not a thing two people can give each other simultaneously!

Professional masseurs are famous for their clean, strong hands, without calluses and with well trimmed, smoothly filed nails. Ragged or long nails spoil a good massage. Often a woman will give the man a manicure before the mas sage session begins.

USING A VIBRATOR

Electric vibrators can be used in many ways as a kind of electric massage. These have batteries or electrical cords and are held in the hand. Placed lightly against the skin, they give a pleasant feeling on almost any part of the body and may be used as a help in giving massage to someone else or to yourself.

These devices are sometimes used lightly on the sensitive parts of the body to help arouse sexual feelings. Each lover can explore the partner's body to find places that seem best for this. And, going beyond foreplay or arousal, vibrators are used as part of pleasuring or masturbation. A great many people think vibrators are too noisy, gadgety, and "fake" for genuine lovemaking, and they certainly are an "extra" and not essential to sexual pleasure.

Vibrators should be used lightly and carefully, especially the first time, when the user is finding how they affect him or her. Lightly holding the device *near,* not *on,* the clitoris can be very pleasant for the woman.

You may have seen in a drugstore window vibrators that are made to look like penises. These are really not of much use as a substitute for a penis, because the sensitive areas are near the clitoris and at the entrance to the vagina and just inside it. Other styles of vibrators, which don't look like penises, are probably better for the purpose.

Some men have found it pleasant to have a vibrator touched lightly *near* the scrotum or around the base of the penis, but not on the testicles or the head of the penis.

Anything used to touch the genitals should be kept clean, and that goes for vibrators. Some vibrator users are afraid of electric shocks and prefer the battery-run kind. Others say the battery vibrators don't deliver a strong enough vibration for them.

A vibrator is a machine, not a lover, and it has to be used sensitively by a loving hand. Only a vibrator made for the purpose should ever be used. No one should ever go near delicate human parts with other kinds of powered devices.

SEX IS A FRIENDLY PLEASURE

Recently a letter came from a young woman who wrote, "My lover comes on very strong. When we are hugging and kissing or making love he does a lot of pinching, squeezing hard, scratching and hurting. I think I am supposed to like it because it shows how strongly I affect him, but he gets very rough, and I get the feeling that he likes to hurt and that hurting me gives him pleasure. But it gives me pain and a lot of black-and-blue places."

What she is talking about is something that many lovers enjoy. It is a style of lovemaking that suits some people. But she has a right to complain if she really doesn't like it. Making love is a friendly thing, and lovers should please each other.

Getting a little rough during lovemaking or necking is very familiar. Hickies are well known among sweethearts who like them. Hickies are those little bruises you can get from being kissed a little roughly or nipped a little, and they are not really brutal—just a sign of enthusiasm. Unless the one receiving the hickies doesn't like them.

Some lovers are rather athletic and expect roughhousing with their love. But that isn't the only style of lovemaking, and it is to be used only when both lovers agree to it.

There is a kind of sex play called sadomasochism, in which the partners agree to give and take some real pain. For those who like it, this makes the sexual pleasure more intense, but even those who like it will agree on a signal that means "Please, stop." Of all the lovers in the world, only a few really like this kind of sex play, and you don't have to like it at all. If sweet, gentle touching is all you want from a lover, you have every right to the treatment you prefer.

Sadistic lovers who enjoy sex more when they are giving pain and fear to their partners sometimes get carried away and do real harm. Sometimes their lovers die of the injuries. So if you think there is something wrong with rough sex, and it frightens you, you have good reason to think that.

A lover who can't stop getting too rough for a partner had better be left, at least for a while. It may be that some sessions with a psychotherapist or sex therapist will enable a person of this sort to enjoy a gentler kind of love. But it is not your responsibility to accept hurting, and learning to change behavior is up to the lover who has the problem, not the person who is more a victim than a loved one.

4

Learning About Other People

School teaches subjects like math and English, but even more it teaches people about other people. School is where you share a space and time with all those others. They do different things to you. They talk to you, make you laugh, share with you. And you do your share. Also, people bug you, get in your hair, on your nerves, mess you up. You yourself both please and annoy other people. This is the truth of it. And all of you in that school learn how to get along in life with other people. Some students really get into that life—they eat, sleep, and live it. Others just put up with it. And others duck in and out of it, attracting as little attention as they can.

The shyest person is the one we are most interested in—because the great majority are like that. Almost everybody is shy inside. Wondering if other people really like him or her at all. If his or her act is really any good. That goes for team captains and class presidents as well as for the slide-bys. You will find that out as you get older, but it is ten times more useful to you to know it now.

SO WHAT ABOUT SEX?

"What's all this got to do with *sex*?" you may ask. "What I want to know about is sex, not all this stuff about getting along with people."

Getting along with people is the key to having good sex when the time comes for that. Look—you already have fantasy sex and probably some masturbation. Which does *not* make your eyes weak, drive you crazy, or grow hair on your palms! Real-life, two-person sex happens not in daydreams but in real life, with real people. It happens in the world, where there is friendship, rivalry, getting close to people, and getting mad at people. It's real, like other real things that you can sometimes do right and that sometimes just won't let you do them. So all this about getting along with people is something you will use when it comes to being in love and having sex. Without knowing about real people, you can spoil real-life love very easily. Out of pure ignorance.

What we will talk about in this chapter is not all that hard to handle. You will probably learn these things anyway, just by living. But it helps, it speeds things up, to *think* about what life teaches, to *understand* what it is that you are learning, and to *know* what you know. It makes it easier to put all the puzzle pieces together.

MAKING THE PLUNGE INTO REAL LIFE

Your life at school is your life and it's real. But maybe you don't feel that you are really in it. Or *into* it, as people like to say now.

Well, it is your school life and your young-time, and we say get into it before it goes by. It goes by so fast! Get the most out of it, get the fun out of it. There is a place in it just for you, just for the kind of person you are.

A girl had to enter a new school. She didn't know anyone. Her father said, "So you don't want to join in. At least be an intelligent observer. Stay after classes are over. Look around and see what funny things are going on. Be as aloof as you want to be, but take everything in and tell me about it afterward."

She stayed after school. Everybody was doing this or that. She watched the girls' field-hockey team practice—very mystifying. A woman in a sweatsuit with a whistle came up to her and said, "Play hockey?"

"No."

"Want to be team manager? I need one desperately."

"I don't know anything about it."

"Nobody ever does. You do it first, and know about it after. Stick around and I'll make a bigshot out of you."

So she hung around and for three years she was team manager and had friends and found out how to get to be something just by doing it. She met other girls, went home with them, joined other activities with her new friends, and became part of the school. That beat being an outsider, and it all came from just being where the action was. The life of the school took her in.

Years later she told her father he had given her a great piece of advice, or else conned her into doing what she was afraid to try. He had forgotten the whole thing! But he had done a good thing at the time, and he was very pleased to be told the story.

She really had more fun in other things than field hockey, but she stuck with it anyway. The friendships and the traveling with the team in the bus were the best part, and she got a team jacket that she could wear around the school to show she really belonged.

One thing she learned helped her all her life. She found out that if she was willing to do something, people would want her around. Especially the leaders, the stars, who turned out to be simply just young people like herself. They all needed friends and helpers. So she always had something to do and she always had friends.

Lots of different things happened to her in her school years. She had trouble with some subjects and got easy A's in others. She fell in love twice. One love ended in heartache, and the other got her a male friend who kept in touch all her life. She was disappointed about not getting a part in a play. But she got another part and she did enjoy that. And through happy times and tough times she was always somebody. And she had friends!

She married a man she met at college and became a teacher and an amateur actress and got lots of parts that she *wanted,* from her late twenties on.

LET'S TALK

Sometimes a young person wants to argue with us about all this growing-up advice. Something is bugging him. So we have a talk!

"What's bugging you about all this?"

"Well, like, you keep saying teenagers don't want sex. That other people are pushing them into it. Teenagers are *dying* to have sex! That's why so many of them get into it! Nobody is forcing them."

"Lots of teenagers tell us they are afraid, that they don't want to, that people are pressuring them."

"Why wouldn't they want to have sex when it's such a strong drive?"

"Everybody wants to have sex sometime, but maybe not right now. Very few people want to have it on the bus or the subway, when they are going somewhere else. They want to be in the right place, at the right time, and ready for it. Even with a strong urge to have sex, people can have a strong feeling holding them back. This is a known fact. A person who is too young to be totally in charge of his or her own life, who feels in transit, like being on a bus, is not ready. Not with a real person, who could be taking over, dominating, changing all of life. A girl especially wants to wait until she isn't afraid of those things, and until she has a man who, if she gets pregnant, will regard it as his pregnancy too."

"Not everybody who 'does it' gets pregnant."

"But too many do, and the rest worry about it, so it's too big a deal when you're still chewing bubble gum and maybe sucking your thumb in secret. You know that you don't want to get any girl pregnant. Not yet."

"Yeah, well."

"You know you don't. It's serious and it's a rotten experience. Who needs it?"

"So everybody should just fool around, no intercourse."

"Nobody says fool around. But if you and a girl are going to do something more than just hug and kiss, the only way to be one-hundred-percent sure she doesn't get pregnant is to keep the penis away from the vagina. Petting is something you might find yourself doing, even if nobody says, 'Go to it, with my blessing.' But intercourse at your age is crazy."

"Don't you always say to use contraception?"

"Contraception only lowers the chance of getting pregnant. It isn't one-hundred-percent sure. Intercourse is only for people who can take care of the consequences themselves, the two of them, without wrecking their plans and upsetting their lives and the lives all around them."

"So you say nobody has to fool around, but if they *do* fool around, don't put the penis near the vagina. But if they put the penis near the vagina, use contraception, it at least *lowers* the chance of pregnancy. So, listening to you, somebody gets the idea of having intercourse after all."

"Somebody hearing a hurricane warning will put out to sea in a canoe. I hope they at least wear a life jacket. Some people are going to have intercourse, some people are going to get pregnant, no matter what *anybody* says to them."

"Well, you will be glad to know I'm not planning to make anybody pregnant."

"Bravo!"

BEING ACCEPTED

There is nothing wrong with wanting to be accepted. It's normal! Being accepted makes life with people possible. But you are better off if people accept you as you really are and not for something you have to break your neck trying to be. If some crowd wants you to go beyond your limits, beyond what you are sure you can handle safely, back away and find another crowd. There is always another crowd.

In your crowd they like to dress a certain way, and clothes help you feel okay when people are looking at you. Fortunately, today nobody has to go broke to look okay. You don't have to know a lot about clothes to have a pair or two of jeans, and they are easy to look after and wear.

It isn't always jeans time, though, and most very young people just wear what their parents buy for them, until the day comes when special clothes—prom clothes, church clothes, party clothes, going-out clothes—may have to be more what the young people want than what Mom and Dad had in mind.

A wise parent *helps* the young person find clothes that will be accepted where the young person hangs out, by the young crowd in that school or place. But parents were not put on earth just to be driven crazy, either. Dad will say, "That dress shows too much."

"Everybody wears them like that."

Look, you have to compromise a little. Find something that you can wear with the crowd that won't make Dad's face get purple and his eyes bulge.

But it *isn't* fair when money is spent on clothes that make the young person cringe when somebody looks. Clothes have to be grown-up enough and they have to stay within what the crowd accepts without *upsetting* the parents. That makes life easier for everybody.

Parents may ask you to dress a certain way for visiting Grandma on Thanksgiving, for going to temple or church, for a family trip to an opera or concert. That's fair enough. But for teen places and events, teen clothes.

A mother is always lending. Makeup, accessories, and most of all advice and hem-fixing. Dad can help tie a tie right when the lad wears one only twice a year. Even square parents can be helpful when they are needed.

CLEANLINESS

Girls generally begin to be fussy about clothes before boys do, and also about hair and nails and clean skin. But boys really shape up in the seventh or eighth grades—without being urged. And even little boys are cleaner today than before showers came into most homes. Showers are easy and fun.

Body odor. This begins in puberty or adolescence and it seems to be more dramatic with some people than with others. Some people get away just with showering regularly and changing into fresh clothes daily. There definitely are some people who, after puberty, have a stronger odor than most and who feel more comfortable using a deodorant. That's fine, but only if the deodorant is used *after* a good shower or bath and not *instead* of it.

PIMPLES

Some kids never get them. Others have a lot of them, and there is nothing to be done but keep clean and remember that every high school in the memory of woman or man has had its share of blazing faces. Noticeably, many acned youths are athletic, vigorous, good-natured, and popular. Every youngster who has this condition sees a doctor at least once about it and gets some advice. Every once in a while the condition turns out to be an allergy rash that goes away with treatment.

Neither masturbating nor not masturbating has anything to do with it.

People are very glad to see a high-school student with acne who goes about with a friendly smile, greeting everyone freely without the slightest embarrassment. This is not rare. The unselfconscious young person with the problem is a known type. If you have pimples or acne, notice how many people have it and rise above it.

Young people's marvelous hairstyles change constantly but nowadays you can wear it pretty much any way you like. Since young people have such attractive hair, they can make much of it simply by keeping it full, combed, and shining clean.

Big bucks for weekly trips to the hairdresser for either boys or girls seems a foolish idea to us, but then we, the writers of this book, are Depression kids and we think everything costs too much. The real point is that really beautiful young hair hardly needs a great deal of artificial arrangement. And simple hairstyles go well everywhere today.

A nice custom that seems to have come in the past twenty-five years is that of girls cutting boys' hair for love or friendship. They also do one another's hair. There are many very skillful home hairstylists now. And the price is certainly right.

KINKY CLOTHES AND HAIR

It's fun to wear hair in a kinky way that your own generation likes. Something very trendy or faddy in clothes is fun, too. But if it gets you into conflict, why wear yourself out for a hairdo as if it were a crusade? Because there is a way to have your way and please the old folks too.

Teenage life is full of costume parties and occasions where hair, normally demure, can be put up or colored (with wash-out color) for just a few hours. Or an extreme wig can be worn. The big football game, Halloween, St. Patrick's Day, and many other special occasions are right for a show of high spirits. You can have the fun of looking wild for a while without turning a nice-looking kid into a permanent troll.

FINDING OUT HOW TO DRESS

There is a time for everyone when looking *right* is the desired thing—but how do you do it? Besides having very vague ideas about good style, you are short the hundreds of dollars needed to dress like a fashion model. The idea is to begin to put a wardrobe together bit by bit, occasion by occasion. But what do you buy, and what goes with it? With the nice basic suit or dress, what shoes, tie, handbag, hat, jewelry?

When you want to begin to conform but don't know how, parents may have good advice about buying things and when to wear them. If their ideas are out of line with yours, the thing is to explain how you feel about wearing something that makes you stand out in the wrong way. Parents can understand things pretty well if young people explain how they feel.

Friends will talk to you about clothes and what to wear when. For good ideas, watch what the best dressers in school are wearing. And by the way, making your own clothes can be easy!

HAVING FRIENDS AND BEING USED

"A real friend doesn't *use* you," people may say. But in fact real friends do use each other all the time. That's what friends are for.

The best use a friend puts a friend to is as a friend. We can all use a buddy, a backer-up, a personal cheering section, someone to listen to our troubles. And most friends are more than talk. They borrow and lend from one another, do one another's work sometimes. Who worries about using or being used?

The time may come when someone really does seem to be getting too much in return just for letting you hang around waiting to do another errand, chore, or favor. The person eager for friendship can be misused by the one who really doesn't need a friend as much as a servant. And in return for being accepted, the eager one may have to get into sex, drugs, or theft. When this kind of thing seems to be coming up, it is time to pull out of this bad friendship.

You can't count every candy bar lent and every favor done, looking for an absolutely fair exchange, but a good friendship is good for you and a bad friendship makes you unhappy and gets you into trouble.

But sometimes it may not *look* like a fair exchange between friends to outsiders, while only the friends themselves can really know. We know a pair of women who met in high school and were friends for sixty years. And people said one was taking more out of the friendship than the other—sometimes it was one, sometimes it was the other! One woman was careful, steady, and precise, and the other was flighty, emotional, and amusing. Who could measure what the steady one gave the other in sensible help, or what the other added in fun to the sensible one's life? The outsiders were wrong.

But if a friend ever complains about being short-changed on friendship, that feeling should be respected. Maybe one person *does* always do the borrowing, and maybe that same person is always the one who goes for the Cokes. And maybe it only *seems* like that to the complainer. But it is how it seems that counts most, isn't it?

For a pal, one can try to change one's habitual act a little.

EVERYBODY IS A CHARACTER

One thing shows up in a gang of friends who hang out together for a long time. Each person has a character that is not going to change basically, though he or she can shape up and improve in certain ways. Lazy, stubborn, quick-tempered, uncomplaining, show-offy, teasing, bossy. Something. The quick-tempered one may learn to soften the answers, the lazy one may learn to get a lot of work done in a day, but underneath, the character is still there, just mellowed out a good deal. In the gang, each person's character gets to be known. And plenty may be said about that character, but in fact everybody comes to accept it—even the person who has it! In a good gang, all the characters learn how to talk, argue, persuade, and amuse one another. When to tease and when to lay off. When and how to cheer one another up.

People don't join a group or gang to learn about people and getting along with them. They drift into a group hoping for friends to have fun with and do things with, for company and entertainment. Or they get into a group because life puts them there—a class in school, for instance, or a place where people work together.

Most youngsters belong to more than one group. You can belong to your class at school, to a small group of buddies in the school, to the school band where you play trombone, to the camera club, to the youth group at church or temple, to a little gang of grown-ups and newspaper-delivery kids at the local newspaper office, to the gang in your home neighborhood, and to a swimming-hole group of summer kids and farm kids upstate. Maybe the home neighborhood gang sees less of you than they used to because you felt they were all trying too hard to get into trouble you didn't need. So you pal around with farther-from-home groups now.

One girl got into a neighborhood gang when she and her family moved in. She was 12. And she was crazy to be accepted and make friends. She did whatever they wanted to do in order to belong. Then, when she was 14, she had a scare—or three scares. She got picked up for shoplifting, had her face smashed in a car accident riding with a teenager, and got pregnant. She couldn't say which of three boys was the father. She had a miscarriage in early August and went back to school in September. Her parents made her join a church group, which was a good idea that might have worked and might not have worked. As it happened, it *did* work. At first she hated that bunch, but then she liked it, and eventually she became a fanatic member of it and would talk about nothing else. The church group wasn't made up of saints. One boy knew about her and tried to have sex with her! In the parish house! But after her scares it was easy to say no. Her face looks great again, and she belongs to a school drama club, a ballet class, a group who stuff envelopes for a political club, and the school ski club. She was lucky that she found a lot of people who liked her and didn't think she should trade sex for being allowed to hang around.

BEING A LONER

Some people are labeled as loners because they don't seem to be part of any group. They go off by themselves and seem to like it. Around other people they are reserved. Very often this type of person will surprise somebody by an unexpected act of friendship. A friend in need is a friend indeed, yeah, but this sort of person seems to be a friend only if you are indeed in need. It is a mistake to call this a cold sort of person. But maybe you never get close to him or her, either.

Inside, everybody feels like a loner now and then, outside of all the groups, even those the person belongs to. This feeling comes and goes.

There are also people who are not true loners but who have only a few close friends. This may be true wherever they land, away at college as well as at home. In the army, or in the city they move to because of a job. They always find one or two particular friends. And they read or work on a hobby a lot by themselves.

AND THEN THERE ARE PEOPLE ADDICTS

People addicts go bananas when they are alone even for a little while. They want someone around night and day. They can't stand silence and empty rooms. They like jobs where they work with people, and they like cities where they can always see a human being wherever they look. After work, they want a hangout where people get together sociably.

Sometimes they wear their friends out a little, but they are very likable because their problem, if that is what it is, seems so human.

When they are alone they listen to radio or tapes or keep the TV going. Even while they are reading. To them, the singers and actors and writers are friends for when no live, warm friend is handy. They can get mountains of work done if they have people around; they are energetic and work hard.

And they are great when *you* feel lonely, because if you call them up and say, "Can I come over, or can you come over here?" they shout "Great!"

A LITTLE MORE ABOUT USING PEOPLE

Some people get tagged as "users" because they have to lead, it has to be their show, they make *you* listen, and what they want you for is to be part of their act. But since you can get something out of them, too, it doesn't have to be a one-way street.

Group leaders, team captains, and club leaders tend to be like that. And there are grownups who really love the group of kids they teach or coach or lead. Coaches, drama teachers, dance teachers, music teachers, and Scout and Y leaders may be like this.

Sometimes they seem to be too much, but you have to see that without them there might be a lot of fun missing from life. And young people learn game, hobby, and work skills from them. If it weren't for these "users," there might be no team, no school play, no band, no choir, no dance class.

If the time comes when you think you have had enough of their thing, they may look at you as if you have betrayed them. You have to think hard about staying with them or going on to something else. Your decision.

We repeat, these people may be kids or grown-ups.

They are very useful, because while you are learning their thing and having their kind of fun, *you* are using them, right?

FANTASY, GOOD AND BAD

Everyone has a fantasy life. Some of it comes ready-made in books, movies, or TV. Some you can claim for your very own, though most of our fantasies or daydreams are partly ready-made and partly our own imagination.

Fantasy, or daydreaming, is very useful. You may be daydreaming and there will come to you a very good idea for how to do something. You connect a certain pile of used lumber and a fence or shack you would like to build. Or you get a good idea to use in an English composition.

But fantasy isn't just useful. It can be beautiful just for itself. It can be a way of relaxing when you are too wound up to go right to sleep.

Fantasy dresses up real life. A tree to some people is just something to hang a sign on or to try not to hit with a car because it's hard. But fantasy makes a tree special to you. Something beautiful and alive. Like you. Fantasy helps you put a certain glamour into your own life and the life of friends. Without imagination, there is no glamour. Human life needs it.

Bad fantasy leads to bad mistakes in life. For instance, TV is largely manufactured fantasy, but you can think that what you see there will work in real life. But it is full of fantasy ideas about violence and sex that spell trouble (T-R-U-B-B-L-E!) if you try to act that way.

In stories and in commercials, TV is always showing people meeting, seeing clothes and hair and faces and bodies, then jumping into bed to have sex.

If you try that in real life, you can get turned down a lot, or you can spend a lot of time in unhappy, painful relationships with the wrong people. TV love and sex don't show enough of coming to be friends with someone, finding how well the two of you can make it together, slowly getting closer. Like two real people instead of two fantasy figures.

In TV fantasy, problems are solved with guns and fists, and lovers don't share work and ideas but go on and on making each other jealous, breaking up and making up over hokey love problems. All this is fun and harmless if you don't take it for reality.

Pornography is fantasy, too. It may look very real because you see bodies, breasts and behinds, penises and vulvas, people having different kinds of sex. And that looks like the real thing to you, so it seems very vivid and real. But porn is mostly male fantasy about guys with big penises that are always hard. Ejaculating what looks like pints of semen but is really a movie effect. And the women are sex robots who do whatever the male fantasy asks of them. Real females are less likely to cooperate in that way! Real women and men have to please each other, and that takes time and understanding.

Everybody has the right to know that other people want to have sex too, if the whole picture is right. But real sex is a two-person deal, not a masturbation fantasy like porn.

If your head is full of ideas about how a lover *must* look and act, you may skip right over some wonderful person who would make you very happy. If only you had gotten your ideas from observing real life and living it! Instead of watching those look-alike actors and actresses earning their salaries in front of the camera.

THE MIND CONTROLS IT ALL

Signals for sexual arousal come from the brain. And the brain can control sexual behavior. Penises and clitorises don't boss people around; the mental habits people have do that.

So you can give yourself time to learn about two-person sex and love before plunging into it. Deep involvement with another can be put off for years while you learn about all the different ways of liking, loving, and living with friends and group members.

The group is a great class for learning about relationships and people. But not everybody has to be a real group joiner. You can drift in and out, having fun here and there, without being a full-time member of anything.

It is good to have more than one group to fall back on. Then, if things go a little sour in one group, you don't have to stick around being the goat or doing things you would rather not do. Or even putting up with people who are being a pain.

Groups may develop a style you just don't like. Even if it isn't really dangerous. If you have somewhere else to go, it makes backing away that much easier.

You can definitely use your own mind to decide about groups and about dating some one person. Here is one way groups are very helpful. Starting to date can be awkward until you get the knack of asking somebody for a date, not minding if the answer is cool or a definite no. Until you have that kind of confidence, you can use group membership to get next to somebody without making a bold move. What you and the other person do in the group you just might do by yourselves sometime. And if that feels good, it can turn into dating for a while.

The other person may feel better about getting into dating by degrees. First *in* the group, then apart from the group. And a girl in particular is apt to trust a boy more if he is part of some group she knows. He isn't a stranger from who knows where, coming up to her and suggesting who knows what, but a regular guy known to people she knows.

And if you are with a person as group members you can back out more easily if you decide you want to.

SOME RULES FOR FRIENDSHIP AND LOVE

Should friendship and love have rules? Shouldn't these personal things be played by ear? Well, people who stay together learn that rules are useful. Each couple develops its own rules.

One couple found a way to have fights and get over them fast. Things would get bad between them and they would go on like this:

"I hate you. I really hate you! I'm sorry!"

"I hate you, too! You really stink! You stink worse than anybody I ever knew. I'm sorry I said that!"

They turned every fight into a series of insults with instant apologies. They were laughing half the time they were fighting. This would not work with every couple.

Here are some rules, not many, for friendships and more-than-friendships.

Have an established way of making up after a fight.

When the old argument comes up about what to do on a date, with a friend or a sweetheart, let one person choose one time and the other person choose the next time. And on small disputes about which way to go, bus or car, or which place to eat, pizzeria or coffee shop, get used to flipping a coin. Get used to enjoying the other person's way and the other person's food. It's broadening.

Listen to your friend. In every dispute about how people should dress, act, think, or about who is better, Redford or Newman, Mick Jagger or one of the Beatles, Godzilla or King Kong, don't always try to shut the other up and press your idea forward. Listen. The friend will like it. And you can learn something if you listen. Friends are always teaching one another.

When there are hurt feelings, always have a rule that one-half the blame belongs to each person. That may sound dumb, but it is nearly always true and it makes it easier to make up. Because nobody has to *crawl*, just take his or her own half of the blame.

A certain couple uses that rule. Listen to her bawling him out, making her point, getting rid of her anger, and making up all at the same time:

"You say I am too touchy, and that's true, okay? I'm too touchy. So I get mad over nothing and we have a whole week spoiled. But I say *you* are selfish and careless and *you* are the one who spoils the week. Okay? At lunch on Friday you said you would call me where I was baby-sitting and figure out Monday night. I waited and waited and no call. So I'm touchy—who likes to think nobody wants to call them up and talk to them? And you *know* I'm touchy, so you should have made a point of calling. It would have taken three minutes to call me up sometime in that whole long evening. So it's half my fault for being touchy and it's half yours for not having the decency to call. So let's try to class up our act, and that's that."

Anybody can admit it was *half* his fault.

5

What Every Teenage Girl Should Know

"Becoming a woman!" That's how some people refer to a girl's first menstruation. Some say it playfully, some very solemnly. But it is hardly sensible to call it becoming a woman when it happens to a child. Most girls begin to menstruate between the ages of 12 and 15. It can come to some girls as early as 9 or as late as 17.

Physically, she can be impregnated. But her body is still immature, and so is her mind—no matter how wise and clever she may be in some ways.

The first menstruation is not a dramatic event like going over Niagara Falls in a barrel. But the girl should know it is coming or it may frighten her. She should understand that it is natural and happens to half the human race, approximately. The female half, which is thought of by many people as the better half.

We know a girl who had no idea her first menstruation was coming. She was away from home at camp and her panties and pajama bottoms kept getting bloody. She didn't understand, so she hid them under her mattress. She was scared and didn't know how to tell anyone. Fortunately, a girl counselor found the hidden clothing. She told the girl what was happening, got her some sanitary napkins and showed her how to wear them, and had the stained clothes washed. Now, that was a totally unnecessary time of fear for the child. She should have been prepared.

Dr. Ruth has the idea that it would be nice to have a party with a cake to celebrate the event, so that happy feelings would be part of the first menstruation. Not to make too much of it, but congratulations might be in order, so the girl doesn't think of her monthly periods as "the curse." Because sometimes the first menstrual period comes when a girl wants to go on skipping rope forever. She resents this intrusion on her little-girlness, and wants to know that her parents are still going to pet her and treat her as their little darling for a long time to come. So, at the same time, a party would show that menstruation is an accomplishment, like being a whole year older.

She may be more a woman than the 9-year

THE FOUR PHASES OF THE MENSTRUAL CYCLE

	Phase 1: Days 1 to 5	Phase 2: Days 6 to 13	Phase 3: Day 14— Ovulation	Phase 4: Days 15 to 28
UTERINE LINING	The uterine lining is shed. Menstruation is taking place.	The uterine lining is beginning to thicken.		The uterine lining breaks down and this is the first day of menstrual bleeding.
OVARIES/ FOLLICLES	The ovaries are producing minimal amounts of hormones.	The ovaries are producing the hormone estrogen. The follicles in the ovary are moving toward the ovary's surface.	The ripe ovum detaches from the ovary and moves into the fallopian tube.	The remnants of the follicle become the corpus luteum and begin to make the hormone progesterone. The progesterone causes the uterine lining to grow thicker. The corpus luteum disintegrates when fertilization does not occur. The disintegration of the corpus luteum means that progesterone is no longer being produced.
PITUITARY GLANDS	The pituitary glands are producing minimal amounts of hormones.	The pituitary glands are producing the hormone FSH.	The pituitary glands release LH, a hormone.	

-old, but she is still maturing. The maturing process includes changes in bone and flesh, organs, emotions, and mind. It goes on into the mid-20s.

Two best friends from grade school on are very likely to mature very differently from each other in details of breasts, hips, body hair, mental outlook, and interest in boys. They will discuss these differences during those long, long sleepover talks, and this is comforting to each of them. And helps them to understand the complex changes taking place.

YOU AND YOUR GYNECOLOGIST

"Wait a minute. I don't *have* a gynecologist." So you are probably thinking right now. But part of growing up for a girl is learning to think about her body and its health, and learning to think easily of going to the gynecologist's office for regular visits.

Probably you are willing to put off any such visit indefinitely. Because, as every gynecologist knows well, many patients dislike the idea. The best that the gynecologist can hope is that his patient is relaxed and knows that nothing terrible will happen there.

What *will* happen there? Well, you take off your panties, lie back on the examining table, and put each foot into a raised stirrup, so that the doctor can examine your genitals. That's not a position you learn in ballet class or charm school! But it is comfortable and sensible for the purpose of a pelvic examination.

What is this pelvic exam for? The gynecologist is looking for lots of things, just as the family doctor does when he looks into your throat, your nose, and your ears and eyes. It is part of a regular health check-up.

A good gynecologist is considerate. You have a right to expect that, and if you ever think it isn't so, you must tell your mother about it. If there is any real discomfort during the exam, tell the doctor about it. And remember that it is *your* vagina, and if you want to you can call off the exam at any point. Don't be bullied about that. A good gynecologist wouldn't want you to be.

During the exam, the gynecologist will tell you what is going on, how it will feel, and to let him know if anything bothers you.

We are going to call the gynecologist "he." You may have a woman gynecologist, but then you may not, and it is just as well to accept the idea of a male gynecologist, because the best one in your area may be a man. And this is a medical thing between you and your gynecologist, not a sexual thing.

When he looks into your vagina he will use an instrument called a speculum. This gently spreads the vagina open for examination, and almost every virgin can be examined without having her hymen broken. A small speculum can be used, and the gynecologist can use it very carefully. Having a hymen on the wedding night is no longer a big deal for well-educated couples, but why damage the hymen for no reason?

The male gynecologist always has a nurse or a woman assistant with him in the examining room during a pelvic exam. That makes him feel more comfortable as well as you.

Of course, you will have a bath or shower before visiting the gynecologist, because your genitals and anus should be clean. No other special cleaning is necessary unless you are told so in advance; the vagina cleans itself very nicely. So you need not be nervous about that.

Girls have worried that the gynecologist can tell if they masturbate. He can't. The appearance of your clitoris tells him nothing, whether you have masturbated two thousand times or never. But as he touches the genitals they may react involuntarily, just as you may gag involuntarily when a tongue depressor goes way back in your throat. The gynecologist expects these reactions and does not comment on them. He will not think that you are being sexually aroused by him.

Before going to the gynecologist you might do your own examination of your genitals, using a hand mirror. You can't see into your vagina very far, but you can look at your inner and outer lips, your clitoris, your urethral opening, where the urine comes out, the entrance to your vagina, and a little way in. It is good for you to have seen this area for yourself before you let someone else look at it. It is reassuring. You know what he is seeing when he is looking "down there."

Somehow, knowing what you're showing makes you less nervous.

TOUCHING DOWN THERE

Parents used to tell girls not to touch themselves down there, and lots of girls obeyed. For boys the warning was more confusing, because on the one hand they were told not to touch their penises and on the other hand they were taught to hold them every time they urinated. (That was so the little men would urinate in the toilet and not all around it!) So the boys knew that nothing would happen from touching their penises, and touching would lead to fondling.

The writers of this book feel very sympathetic to parents! We are parents ourselves. What parents say to children about sex they say to protect the children, doing the best they can with the information they grew up with. That should be understood. If a parent is old-fashioned about some things, that doesn't mean that she or he hasn't learned a great deal that is right and should be listened to. But looking and touching are educational, and masturbating is a private act and does no harm. It can do good. A girl can learn to have orgasms that way, which will mean that she never has to worry about whether she is capable of having them. And what she learns about pleasuring herself she can teach to a husband or lover when the time comes.

A girl might curiously explore the sensations around her anus with her finger. No harm. But she should wash her hands before going near her genitals, because organisms that live harmlessly in the bowel can cause infections in the vagina. These can be cleared up with medicine prescribed by a doctor, but vaginitis is uncomfortable and should be avoided. Lovers may sometimes touch the anus with finger or penis, but they must wash that finger or penis before going near the vagina with it.

YOUR BODY AND HOW TO WEAR IT

Some girls can slump appealingly, but the best way in general is for the girl to stand straight and inflate the lungs fully. There is no use in trying to hide her breasts when they begin to push out her blouse. Many girls do this whether they feel their breasts are too big, too pointy, too small, or whatever. Whatever they are like, let her display them. Not bare on the beach, unless it is one of those permissive beaches! But breasts are to be proud of, not to cringe over. They are hers. That's the way she is. Let other people accept them as natural, neither exciting in ordinary circumstances nor in any way shameful.

During puberty and adolescence breasts change. This year may be the last year that the girl's chest looks like a boy's. But if she is flatter than the Hollywood ideal she is still capable of being desired.

Males praise breasts in their conversation, their poems, and their stories. And they praise many kinds. They are most inspired by the special kind of breasts that their girl friends have. "Ah! Those delicate little breasts!" And so on. They also like very big ones and some whose size is more apparent to the hand than to the eyes.

This happens. A man falls in love with a woman, noting nevertheless that her chest is not mountainous. Sometimes he wishes her breasts were a little bigger. Then one day or night she undresses in his presence and he sees that she has the kind of breasts that are best seen bare. She is one of those who look loveliest nude.

A man can be enslaved by a woman who is as flat as Nebraska.

It works magic to be absolutely unselfconscious about them, whatever their size.

A woman with big breasts will sometimes wish they were smaller, as when she carelessly pinches them while shutting a drawer. She may be admired by big-breast-hunting men, but at times like that she doesn't really care!

Of late there has been a movement to appreciate more kinds of female form. Short, stocky, lanky, voluptuous, wide-hipped, snake-hipped, big-shouldered—all sorts. Artists have always been more grateful for the variety of women's bodies than for Barbie Doll sameness.

Body worshippers love the Olympics, with the great show of fine bodies of every style. The slender gymnasts! The figure skaters with powerful round thighs! The speed skaters, with *heroic* thighs, in their skin-tight speed suits! It makes a body-watcher's smorgasbord.

No one has ever drawn up satisfactory rules about what attracts or excites men. The nearest anyone has come to it is the man who said that whatever his loved one looks like is what he praises to the skies.

You inherit your basic body as far as skeletal structure and flesh distribution go. If yours is not like your mother's body type, it is like that of some other female ancestor. So what you have is of your family, tribe, or ethnicity. Be proud of it!

You can make the most of your physique by eating sensibly and exercising. No crazy dieting! Good food and exercise will firm up your flesh and make your skin glow and your eyes sparkle.

"Oh, if I could look like Twiggy, though," sighs a nice chunky girl.

Twiggy is lovely. But she is an example of how an extreme type, generally regarded as unfortunate, can be adorable. When she first appeared before an astonished public she was *emaciated*. It showed how an underfed kid could make a hit. But she is not to be imitated unless you have her body type. One man blames her for the wave of anorexia nervosa in young women. "Saint Anorexia," he calls her. This fellow is a speed-skating fan. "Thin Thighs in Thirty Days!" he says. "Who wants *thin thighs*?" To him, thin thighs are like warm ice cream or a rainy day on vacation. Different men like different kinds of bodies, and the same men like different bodies, too—depending on who is wearing the bodies.

Here is something to do whether you already like your body or have your doubts about it. Now, don't think this is nuts until you have tried it! Go to a mirror, dressed or nude. Look at yourself adoringly and say, "Oh, you delicious thing! You must be real, 'cause nobody could have dreamed you up!" Do that whenever you see a mirror. Invent other good things to say, such as, "You and me, baby—all the way!" and, "Who could resist you?" This may start jokingly, but the positive feeling for yourself will infect you, and the infection will spread to other people.

Once a week you might write a short story about a girl just like you, with your face, shape, and character, and how lovable she is and what great things she does in her art studio, in outer space, on the Riviera. Make it short, on one side of a sheet of paper. That way, you won't resist doing it every week. Have men climb rivers and swim mountains for you. These ideas about yourself will stick to you and affect the way you show yourself to other people.

These exercises in confidence-building aren't self-deceitful. The fact is that you are a girl, and girls are desirable and admirable.

Exercise your ability to think well of yourself, and put yourself in the shoes of a male who, for good reason known to him, adores you. Understand how his mind would work to make the most of every little charming thing about you.

WHEN THE GIRLS GATHER

When a group of girls gathers there is likely to be a great deal of talk about clothes, makeup, bodies, hair, and general style. We don't say they won't talk about the nuclear arms race too, but even intellectual women talk "girl talk." Is there anything wrong with it? And when the girls gather there is often some chatter about boys and men.

A lot of useful information gets around by way of gossip. Gossip was the first newspaper and newscast. You hear how this boy got pushy on a date with that girl, how the guys all got the word that a certain person was an easy lay, when in fact she wasn't at all, and much else that relates to your real world, the world of your school and your set of friends.

You don't have to lose your self-respect by the way you take part. You hear mistaken ideas about people, of course. But you can say, "I don't think he is really like that." And you can correct some mistaken idea about sexual development, pregnancy, and so on. So that good information is passed around as well as fluff!

WHAT THE BOYS WANT

Girls are interested in this. Boys seem to give confusing signals about what they *want*. Or they seem disappointing in that they don't seem to want anything. What *do* they want?

"Some boys are really more interested in your mind!" says a girl. And there is a dead silence while the others react to that. And the girl who said it becomes a little defensive. "Well, it's true!" she says, saying it a little louder to make it more true.

One of the other girls is frightened by the remark. Her own mind, she fears, is a mess. If a boy could see into it he would walk away.

Another is skeptical. Boys are one-idea monsters. All they see are boobs and behinds!

Another wishes the subject would change. Boys bore her. She is going to wait until they all turn into men.

Another knows she is bright, and she is thinking about a quiet boy she knows. She hopes it is true that some boys are interested in girls' minds, and that this boy will pay attention to hers.

Another is miffed by the suggestion that there is something better than being great-looking. *She* is great-looking, and that is what boys ought to go for, as far as she is concerned.

These girls are all pretty friendly to one another and might pair up for this or that any afternoon. But they have different ideas about themselves and boys. They are all learning about having friends and acquaintances and boyfriends and *boyfriends*.

What *do* boys want? That's a mixed bag, too. For every girl in that group there is a boy whose ideas roughly match hers. This makes learning about boys a subject that will take more than any school year to learn.

WHAT OLDER PEOPLE HOPE FOR GIRLS

A girl's parents hope that she won't hook up too intimately with any one boy for a while, and that the boys she does hook up with, for now, are not so crazy to have sex as to endanger their daughters. And parents are afraid of boys who have bad problems, because a girl is likely to be oversympathetic and get drawn into the boy's troubles. Too much of her adolescent life can be devoted to defending and comforting him when what he needs is professional help.

Professional educators and counselors (like the writers of this book) meet a teenage girl and try to really understand her. And they hope that her unavoidable encounters with boys will be happy and helpful to her. If she is a virgin, a technical virgin, or a former virgin, they hope the best for her and try to see her as a growing person. That means running some risks and coming out fine. They want her to be open to life and still have a strong instinct for self-preservation. And they hope her strong sexual drive and her strong mothering instinct won't lead her into taking on a boy's problems so much that she doesn't give enough time to her own development.

HOW TO TAKE ADVICE

In real life, the advice you get may come from someone who seems very ordinary, who has funny mannerisms, and who does not in your opinion cut much of a figure. But listen to the advice; listen to see if it makes sense to you and if you can take it.

Often you may seek advice from someone more apart from you than your family. Someone who looks at your situation more coolly and helpfully. That is not a bad idea.

Just being apart from a problem helps to see it sensibly. When professional counselors come to their own children they can turn into just as big panickers as any other mom and pop. Knowing this, they often refer their own kids to someone else for help.

You yourself know that you can sometimes give better advice to other people than to yourself.

So when an older person gives advice, remember that old saying, "Do as I say, not as I do." You can get good advice from someone whose style or performance is faulty.

Every Olympic gold medalist has a coach. How often is that coach a gold medalist himself? Or herself?

Often, good advice comes from very quaint sources.

Even your own parents can give good advice at times!

GIRLS AND BOYS TOGETHER

Girls need to meet boys and have friendships with them, at the very least to learn a little bit about how the other half lives. But girls are rightly frightened of this, and often disappointed when they make friends with boys. And confused. Why can't a girl have the kind of ideal date she dreams about? Why is it always a trade that doesn't come off? Something the girl doesn't want to give in return for something she doesn't really want?

She dreams of romantic evenings from novels. Champagne, moonlight, a light pressure of lips to dream about later. What she is offered is a soda or sundae on the greasy blacktop, and for this she may be expected to give very real petting or sex.

Different things happen with boys. One boy is not sexually aggressive, but, perversely, she thinks he is a wimp. She falls in love with another boy and to some extent becomes involved with him sexually. She finds out he really wasn't interested in *her*, only in sex and in making a reputation as a macho guy. That she finds humiliating.

What is this about boys being sexy but unfeeling?

A boy may be a nice guy, but girls attract him and he has a powerful sex urge. He wants a sweetheart, he wants sex. But he has dreams of getting out into the big world. Learning a trade or a profession that will keep him working hard without much pay for several years, so that marriage or a serious relationship is more or less out. Or perhaps he just wants to bum around awhile, or join the navy and see the world. Or he has playboy ideas about living on a large scale and never settling down.

A boy may belong to an all-male crowd and want to look good to his friends. In that crowd you get points for being athletic, risking life and limb, trying liquor and drugs, and scoring with girls. When you have a little success with a girl, or just spend a harmless evening with her, the idea is to tell all to the boys. Exaggeration is nearly always involved.

The boy may be strongly sexed but very selfish. This is true of many attractive and effective males.

Girls often feel driven into the company of the boys their parents fear. The boys their parents like are so much into sports and schoolwork, computers or music or something like that, that they spend no time with girls. The girl-minded boys are less bright, less self-directed, more openly out to enjoy female company. To parents these young fellows seem to have TROUBLE and PREGNANCY written all over them. But to the girls they are the only boys paying any attention.

Before a girl gets into regular dating with boys, she should have a clear notion of what boys are apt to want and a very definite notion of what she will and will not do on a date. So when the moment comes to be firm, she can do it lightly and with authority.

Boys, remember, are taught to be aggressive in sports and in school and in careers. This carries over into their relations with girls. Not all boys are *ruthless*, however!

YOUR SCHOOL FOR A MAN

The French playwright Molière wrote a funny play about a man who thought women were being raised to be treacherous, so he decided to raise one for himself. To educate her from girlhood to be his perfect mate. The play was called *School for Wives*. The hero found out that you can't force anyone into *your* mold; women, like men, have to be accepted for what they basically are.

But in every happy union of man and woman, each helps to bring the other one up. To love you don't have to think that the person is exactly what you want in every last little nitpicking detail. You love him as he is, and you take over bringing him up where his parents and teachers left off. And he does that for you.

In long, happy marriages the two people keep their own identities, their own personalities, but they absorb a lot of vision and knowhow from each other.

You don't have to look at every boy as potentially yours. But you can look at every boy as potentially *somebody's*. That is practice for sizing up a boy's potential, what he is going to be when he has grown up a bit more. What could a good woman make of that semi-raw male? What would he bring to a marriage? Good sense? Capacity for hard work? Faithfulness?

Entertainment? A sense of adventure? Deep affection?

Playing this game as you look at boys can help you to get a sensible way of thinking about them. And, in the long run, a kind way of thinking about them. It helps to know how to feel kindly toward the male sex. To understand that they aren't perfect heroes, but that they can get closer and closer to that. And in the meantime you can enjoy them for what they really are.

TRADING SEX FOR FAVORS

Friends do each other favors, but when friends trade favors there *is* friendship behind it all. It is not a question of paying for company with favors.

Girls often think that to be popular they have to be foolishly generous. It is chancy to let a boy have sex with you to get his company or to keep in with his crowd of cronies. You are so often short-changed on the deal.

A girl who knows she is desirable sometimes will put a price on her body. You should certainly think your body is valuable, but it is hard to put a price on it. You are not merchandise but a person, and the boys and men you have in your life are not purchasers but people. You need a person, and you need to be needed. When you trade sex for car rides, dinners, shows, for being in the right crowd, you are not being a person and you are not getting the company of a person. It's as if other people were doing the whole deal, and you are on the outside.

CASUAL SEX

There are a great many people who will have sex with any presentable person just for the physical pleasure and the sense of being desired in that way. It would be hypocritical to say that sex for itself alone, casual sex, destroys everybody who tries it. But it has real dangers, and not just V.D. or unwanted pregnancy.

In very young people casual sex leads, oddly enough, to feeling unwanted and undervalued. Boys may want to "do it," and they will "do it" *with* you. But they aren't ready to take *you* on. You are no more than the equipment for "doing it." A kind of punching bag.

Often a girl who has fooled around would like to reverse her life and become a virgin again. This is impossible, but she need not be a virgin to be loved. What she has to do is hold off until she does meet somebody who naturally likes her. This means telling some guys that there is no more easy sex with her. They can get rough, mean, and nasty about that, and maybe she will need some help from an older person to send them on their way.

One girl told Dr. Ruth that she wanted to stop having sex for a while but she simply didn't know how to say no. When the guys put the make on her, she reacted like a trained seal.

Saying yes was what she had trained herself to do. Dr. Ruth told her to get to the school nurse or a clergyman and explain that she needed counseling. And in the meantime to practice the conversations leading up to sex in front of her mirror. Run through the boy's speeches and her speeches until it came time to say, "No, Billy. I'm not into that anymore." What you have said many times, in real conversation or in rehearsal, comes out much more easily.

The girl who has been into sex and wants to stop until she is older has lots of trouble about the way she thinks of herself. She has to regain a certain feeling about herself and boys— that she is a person and that they have to like her or else leave her alone. It is for regaining this feeling that the girl really needs counseling and support from as many people as possible.

No one is destroyed by having had some sex. It does not turn anyone into an ex-person. Life still lies ahead, with many happy possibilities, and the present can be enjoyable. But it is too much for a very young person to try to turn her life around without help.

ADULT MEN

Teenage girls come in contact with adult men in the ordinary course of things. Teachers, friends of parents, men who hire them to work in stores, fathers in homes where the girls baby-sit. It's nice when the men are friendly, and no one should expect the worst from every new man. Friendly is often just friendly. Often, such men will talk to a girl about ways to learn and become more employable, to earn higher pay; they often can give advice on colleges or careers. This is perfectly natural. But you can't count on every adult male's behaving with adult restraint.

If you get the feeling that a man is too close, trust the feeling. You will make few mistakes about this. A man knows that he is supposed to stay clear of a young girl, give her space and a clear way to leave the room if she wants to. Pats on the arm or shoulder may be allowed, but the wise man saves them for girls who know him well.

Don't yelp every time there is a possibly accidental touch on breast or behind—it really could be accidental. On the cafeteria line, for instance, or in an elevator, where it is almost unavoidable. But, except in a crowd like that, your breasts, bottom, and crotch, and any other areas that you decide on, are still not for touching or commenting on. Grown men know how to avoid the wrong kind of touching. If they do touch you the wrong way, avoid the men.

If there is an unwelcome touch, and no crowding that makes it unavoidable, it was intentional. Get away from the man.

It is not freaky for an older man to be sexually attracted to a girl in her teens. But it is wrong to show it and wrong to try to have close contact or sex with her.

It is natural for a girl to have a crush on an older man. But it is foolish to try to have any sort of relationship with him outside the student-teacher, worker-boss, child-of-the-house, and friend-of-the-family range. And if the girl gets a little silly, the man's part is to be understanding but to stop any talk or touching that suggests love or sex. It is against the law for a grown man to have love or sex relations with an underage girl.

Nevertheless, some men do risk the law and their jobs by getting girls into empty classrooms, storerooms, basements, and the like. They will pet and kiss, they will try to have sex. These men don't have to look weird or act nutty. They can seem very grown-up and sensible, and they use that to overwhelm the girl. She is embarrassed to speak firmly, to yell, to run out of the room, to push the hand away.

But, if the girl has thought about this situation before it comes up, she will know what to do at the first wrong signal. Get out of the room and get to some friends, or in sight of some other faculty people or hired help. Just get out of there and get home as soon as you can. That will be a signal to the man to leave you alone in the future. If he goes on trying to get you alone, tell your mother about it very calmly and let her phone the principal about the matter, or deal with it in her way.

If it is a man you work for, and being alone with him is likely to be part of the job, you may have to quit.

If it's a man for whom you've been a baby-sitter, get to the next room and to the lady of the house. Ask her to take you home right away! If she tells *him* to do it, ask her to come along or to drive you herself. If this still doesn't help, call home and ask for a ride.

When you've had some kind of experience that involves an approach to sex with an adult, you should review in your own mind exactly what happened before you try to tell the details to your parents. Get straight what he said, what he touched, where you were, and who else was there or close by.

Also, get straight what *you* said and what touching *you* did.

We must remind you that there is always the danger that you might have misunderstood. The danger of misunderstanding is a serious one and is always possible. You can, in such a case, accuse a man whose actions toward you were more in your mind than in reality.

When you think over what happened, be sure that you are not making a mistake. When you accuse a man wrongly, the matter can be extremely serious for him and his family. Accusations by you can be serious for *you* if you are proved wrong or inaccurate.

When you *are* sure that the man has touched you, invited you to touch him, or, in ways beyond just talking, has tried to become sexually intimate with you, then you must report it.

Talk with your mother and father as soon as possible. They will decide whether this is a matter for just the three of you (and the man) to handle, or whether the police should be contacted.

Sometimes a meeting with a juvenile police

officer will make you feel more comfortable. You were not to blame. You didn't invite or encourage this man's sexual acts toward you. When you and your parents go to the police about such an incident, the police may already know of others like it involving the same man. They won't tell you about that, but they can take necessary action when you are willing to cooperate. You can be certain that they will do their best to keep your involvement private when you do.

For you there are two main things: as a young teenager, you do not stay in a situation where a man attempts to have sexual activity with you. When you experience such acts with an adult male, you protect yourself by immediately getting out of the place where you are and reporting to your parents.

There are other such situations that may come up. What about the lifeguard at the pool who may want to give private swimming or diving lessons?

Sometimes it's the visiting uncle, your mother's or father's brother, who comes to stay for a few days in your family's spare bedroom. He catches a glimpse of you in your slip or in your short nightie and after that he becomes very friendly.

A man who visits your mother, her boyfriend, can become interested as much in you as in her. You watch TV together, prepare snacks in the kitchen, munch popcorn together. While you're watching, his arms go around two sets of shoulders. You like him because he brings fun into the house and his friendly ways make your mother happy.

Now you find that he looks in on you after you've gone to bed, for a special good-night kiss. If there's any fondling or tucking you in, your mother needs to know before it gets any friendlier. Your feelings of happiness at having a new man who acts like your father in your house are important, but you need to be sure that it's your mother who interests him most, not you. Sometimes a stepfather gets this way with a young teenager whose mother he has married.

Sometimes sexual invitations and dangers can come from your big sister's boyfriend who suddenly discovers how grown-up you are. An older cousin who once thought you were a baby meets you again after some years and he's amazed! He didn't realize you were growing up, too. And look at you now!

What are male cousins for if not to make sure you are up-to-date in everything, including sex? He's had quite a few girl friends and he knows what young girls are curious about and what someone like you wants and needs: him!

What about when you sleep over at your girl friend's house, just the two of you? Her father, whom you've known over the years as her "old man," doesn't act so old. He offers you some courtesies, as a good host should, prepares the breakfast in the morning, helps you to make up the bed, and tells you how glad he is that you're his daughter's friend. He may show you some "funny" pictures. He surprises his daughter and he worries you. As long as there's nothing further, no private "courtesies," no touching, no accidental bumping, then you can be comfortable. But if the special attentions and the conversation make you feel ill at ease or uncomfortable, then remember not to sleep over at that girl friend's house. Invite her to your place instead.

All the situations we've mentioned could be dangerous to your health, your safety, and your growing up as a woman. We've said that reporting sexual acts to your parents is important and necessary. Of course, if you think you're being tempted to have sex every time a man says you're a pretty girl, take it easy. Adult men will say this and mean it—and nothing more.

SOME SPECIAL CASES

There may be other strangers in your life whose sexual approaches can be more annoying than important. Some men are "flashers"—they show you their penises, usually from a distance. This is their way of getting attention and, maybe, some kind of sexual pleasure. They don't want anything of you, but they get a thrill when they exhibit their genitals and see your reaction.

Again, the thing for you to do is to get out of the situation without saying anything. If he's sitting in a car, just run to wherever you were going. If you can, get the license-plate number and call the police from a safe place.

Some men (and boys) like to look in your window when you are dressing. They hope you will come out of the shower so they can see you in the nude. Such "voyeurs" try to look in dressing rooms, restrooms, and other places where women undress. At home, be sure your shades are pulled down. Don't invite the Peeping Tom to look into your room. If you hear unusual noises outside your window, phone the police. *Don't* go outside to investigate. Be sure you tell whomever is in the house with you about it before you call.

What about the man who comes to sit beside you at the movies when there are plenty of empty seats? If this bothers you and you feel you don't want to invite any "accidental" touchy-feelies, then move to another seat. He may move beside you again. Then you should get up and tell an usher or the manager.

Here is a very good tip: always go to the movies with at least one other person you know well.

Whenever a man you don't know gets next to you and seems too friendly, be very careful to keep yourself in control. *Don't* let him give you a lift home in his car. Say, "Thanks—I have a ride."

Never, never, never hitchhike.

Never go for a cup of coffee unless it's right nearby and there are plenty of other customers there also. ("I really don't want anything, thanks.") And do get closer to other people who look like a family or who are more your own age.

Don't listen to invitations to be a Hollywood star or a fashion model, or a centerfold for a magazine. If you have the necessary talents for such things, ask your parents to get you an agent. Strangers who see you in a public place are just that—strangers! Get away from them. Even if such a talent scout never says a word about sex, get away.

Girls and women receive obscene phone calls from boys or men. Someone calls you up, asks about your sexual interests, talks about your body, suggests you do sexual acts, and just goes on with this kind of talk. He may whisper to disguise his voice or to sound very threatening. You might know him if he spoke clearly, but usually you don't know him. He may not even know you, but he has made a call and gotten a female voice on the line. Anyhow, he's got your number now. If the phone rings and your father or your brother answers, he'll hang up. If you or your mother or sister picks up the phone (or even your grandmother!), the caller will start giving his little talk.

First, hang up. He may call you right back— remember, he's got your number. In that case, lay the phone down and let him talk to himself until he's exhausted. If you listen, he may describe how he's now masturbating and he'll invite you to share that with him. Just put the phone down and don't answer in any way.

If you can, get to another phone and report this call to the police. It might be traced and he may be arrested. If not, talk this over with your parents and see if changing to an unlisted number is a good idea. It may be a nuisance for a while, but which nuisance do you prefer? For sexual information or stimulation, you don't need your obscene phone caller! To make a number change, the phone company will cooperate. Your next listing should be with initials only and no address if the phone is yours and not for the whole family.

Remember not to join your obscene caller in his conversation, not even to tell him that you know who he really is. You probably don't, and there is no point in playing games. Don't blow a whistle in his ear—he could do that to you the next time he calls. Protect your own privacy and keep such trivial matters from being too important to you.

INCEST DOESN'T MEAN HE LOVES YOU

You have probably heard the word *incest,* which means sexual activity between members of the same family. Most often incest involves father and daughter. Research tells us that this kind of sex takes place more frequently than any other form of incest, such as between mother and son or brother and sister.

Fathers who may get the feeling that they are not wanted by their wives may reach for some kind of comforting from their young daughters. When parents quarrel or disagree or hate each other, the father may feel that his daughter, at least, still loves him. Usually, when families are in some kind of turmoil, the daughter does still love her father. Upsets in the family do not have to result in loss of love between parent and child.

In such situations, the father may spend more time with his daughter. He may come to her bed just to kiss her good-night and may sometimes stay to have her reassure him of her love.

Feeling unhappy and upset, they are comforted by their new sympathy for each other when there is family disagreement. They hold on to each other, cuddle, maybe kiss, and soon the father may become sexually aroused. The daughter, out of her loyalty and sympathy, or from fear of displeasing her father, may accept his fondling and sexual touching. When he attempts intercourse, she knows this is wrong, but her fear and anxiety now cause her to tolerate and accept sex with him. She says nothing to anyone, certainly not to her mother, who she feels may be somehow to blame for what has happened. The girl now realizes that she carries a secret that she cannot share with anyone.

The daughter may continue to accept her father in sexual acts and she may find that there is now a kind of "peace" in the family. Her mother, knowing about the incest in the family or not, is no longer such a target as she used to be for her husband's abuse and complaints. He doesn't "hate" her anymore.

The other children in the family may not notice anything, except that this daughter is now a favorite over all others. They may see or hear the father going into her room, but nothing is said.

In some families this incest may go on for years. The daughter is torn between protecting her father and guarding her life. She doesn't date anyone; her father is jealous and prohibits this. She doesn't take part in the usual social activities that others her age enjoy in school or in the neighborhood. She may never be able to enjoy a normal social life, fall in love with a young man her own age, or experience the kind of sex in her life that she should.

She is quiet in all she does, protecting their guilt and their secret. The daughter is a victim of criminal sexuality and child abuse. She continues in this way until maybe the mother has had enough, or a neighbor may observe certain expressions or intimate actions that don't seem to belong in a family.

A teacher may become interested in the daughter. She is much too quiet, bright but not really doing well. She has no friends her own age—and so on. The teacher may talk over her observations with a school nurse or a counselor. They then decide how to go further for the sake of the young teenager.

The problems of sexual abuse and incest are very serious, even when they don't include bodily violence beyond sexual acts. The girl must be protected as soon as possible. If she is very young, say age 9 or under, her mother is responsible for putting a stop to the incest. She may be able to end it and to keep it within the family, or she may have to go to the police for help. She must do all she can to save her child's mental and physical well-being.

If the child in a case of incest is a young teenager, she must help her mother to end the incest and get good counseling for the family. Including the father.

In case the mother is too afraid or confused to know what to do, the girl must act on her own. She should talk to the school nurse or with a counselor about the problem. The nurse or counselor will know what has to be done. The girl's situation will be kept quiet; people at school won't know, and it won't get into the papers. The girl will be protected and helped to get over the experience.

Usually the members of a family are unable to deal with an incest problem. They need the help of specialists, juvenile-department officers, and counselors.

Girls reading this should bear in mind that there are many very decent men in the world, worthy of trusting and knowing. Most adult men are happy in their own lives and will not want to be sexually involved with you. Most fathers love their children in the right way, and when something goes wrong between themselves and their wives they don't reach for their daughters. Incest and child abuse are facts of life, but so are all the wholesome, happy, rule-obeying families.

When a young person, girl or boy, first thinks about sexual dangers in the real world, there is apt to be a feeling of sickness and fear. The picture of a nice world has been dirtied. This fades away. It is still a pretty world, but we all have to use our good sense to keep our own relationships controlled and on a happy road. And to know in advance exactly what we are not going to do or to allow others to do to us.

We will discuss this matter more in another section on incest later on in the book (page 179).

HAVING A NICE DAY—AND HAPPY TEEN YEARS

People tell you to have a nice day. But is it really up to you? What if there's a math test that day?

Well, you may have kept up with the math pretty well, and the test had the right problems for you, so it turned out to be a nice day after all—only the morning before the test might have been less stomach-achey if there had been no test at all, or if you had *really* kept up with the math homework and *wanted* to take the test.

No day is a really nice day if you aren't ready for it. And while you can be ready for a math test, there are other things that make a rotten day, and that's all there is to it.

One girl we know had an aunt who was a pain. When this aunt came to visit it was a bad day, no matter how many people told her to have a good one. The girl tried to develop a good attitude toward this aunt, but the aunt could *get* to her no matter how good an attitude the girl worked up. When this aunt was visiting, the girl was *so* glad to get out of the house and go to school!

"Aunt Vi had a good effect on me, really," the girl says. "She made me appreciate going to school. Also, all the days and evenings she wasn't visiting, those were nice times."

There are days a girl just never enjoys. Girls who have sex and have to worry when their periods are late have rotten days, and having people say, "Have a nice day, honey," only makes them worse. It is also a rotten day when a girl finds out she definitely is pregnant, and no chance in the world of being 21 instead of 15, of being married instead of being the ex-girlfriend of a 15-year-old boy, of being away from home and able to deal with this herself. It is a rotten day when she finally tells Mom and it gets worse when Pop hears about it.

Nowadays people have more heart for a girl who has an unwanted pregnancy than they did a hundred years ago, but she has a lot of days when "Have a nice day!" hits her like a blow. There's the day she visits the doctor and gets all the advice about this pregnancy she doesn't want. Or there is the day of the abortion, which is not like being run over by a train but is no fun either. The day she gives birth and never sees the baby because it is up for adoption is a poor day, although she may to some extent be glad to have it all over with. And on any day through the whole pregnancy she may see other kids laughing along the street, out of trouble and having a really *peachy* day. That's a bad day for her, too.

Millions and millions of teenage girls avoid these rotten days. Virgins don't have them; technical virgins don't have them. Give yourself a break. Don't you have them, either. Instead, have a *nice* day! Have a lot of them, all through your happy teenage years.

6

What Every Teenage Boy Should Know

Boys talk among themselves about sex and girls because the subjects are important and boys need to learn about them. Of course, there are boys who avoid talking about sex and girls, for various reasons, and this is simply a matter of personal feeling. Nobody has to discuss these matters with anybody. There are other ways to learn.

As for you boys who do talk about these things among yourselves—you are in the majority and there is nothing wrong with this talk. But please understand that your friends are all talking about these things because the subject is interesting. Not because the boys really know much about it.

People under the age of 15 are famous for having very poor information about sex. Inaccurate and harmful *mis*information! So, for your own sake, get the information you count on from reliable people. Your parents, your teachers, your doctor. Or from a reliable book like this one.

You may know an older boy who is a hero to you. He can teach you sports, model building, computer operating, a lot of good things. He may have some tips on dating, dancing, and talking to girls. But he can be mistaken about sexual information.

ANOTHER WAY TO GET BAD INFORMATION

There is another way to get bad information. You look at yourself and you look around at the other males your age and a little older. Your body, your body hair, and your penis and testicles are not just like somebody else's. You may feel funny about undressing in the locker room because of this. Shouldn't you be bigger, leaner, stronger, hairier, with bigger genitals and a deeper voice? Are you really, well, *normal*?

Or maybe you are very big for your age and people seem to expect more of you than they should. You feel 13. Your *are* 14. You look 18. Big girls say things to you about love and you wish you weren't such a freak.

You have bad information if you think that you should look like somebody else at your age.

Boys develop in spurts. Now the body grows, now the genitals. Now the hair sprouts on arms, chest, thighs, and pubic area. It isn't an even growth, all in harmony. And all the boys don't grow together, like a field of wheat. The sizes, colors, and shapes of penises and testicles make a wild variety—all of which are normal.

THE SIZES AND SHAPES OF PENISES

Some penises are short and thick, some are long and thin, some are big when they are hanging down and some get big when they are hard and erect. These variations don't mean much when it comes to being a good lover. It happens that some men with big penises have a lot to learn about pleasing a woman during sex, and some fellows with smaller penises are really better at it. But the place for learning about that is in private with a female partner, not in the locker room or while skinny-dipping with male friends.

Almost every time we hear from some boy or man that he is afraid his penis is small, we find out that some friend teased him about it in the locker room, the shower, or at the beach. It was never a girl or woman who started him worrying about it, but another guy. Some friends!

Anybody who comments on your genitals puts himself in the wrong. After that, he has to prove that he isn't a mean, ignorant, and klutzy character. You yourself must learn never to make cracks about anyone's penis. It's a thing that causes many men unnecessary worry, and it has nothing to do with how good a lover a man is.

Women who are unhappy sometimes complain about their poor sex lives with husbands who don't take enough time making love to them, or don't make love to them often enough. But these women complain about their man's performance—not the size of his penis. If the penis is long enough to reach the outer third of the vagina, it will reach all the sensitive area there is, that any penis can reach. On the other hand, a penis can be too large to go all the way inside a vagina. That isn't a tragedy, either, but it shows that having a very large penis has its drawbacks.

Having a good sexual experience with a woman comes after the couple have learned how to please each other and feel relaxed and confident in bed with each other. This is very important, and the size of the man's penis is not.

During your youth your body will change, and not at the same rate as other fellows' bodies. When you are mature, your body type will be what you inherited from your family. Some woman will love you and your body. And you don't have to please all the women in the world with your body, your penis, or your performance— just the woman who wants to make love with you.

THE COMPETITIVE MALE

Boys are urged to compete. And they want to compete. So, okay! Compete! Be sure to compete at the things you do best—math or tennis or whatever it is. And try competing for fun at everything that comes along, from video games to making the funniest faces at a party. But don't try to make a competitive sport out of love and sex. Sex and love are private, personal, and noncompetitive. A great sexual encounter with a girl or woman you love is more like singing a song, harmonizing, or two people helping each other to build something, or just doing all they can to make each other feel wonderful.

BOYS AND BRAGGING

When males get together they tend to brag about battles they have fought and glorious love and sex conquests. This is especially true when the males are young and still establishing themselves. The bragging may be partly kidding, but it is always partly serious, too.

When you hear a boy tell how he had sex with some girl, don't swallow the story whole. You don't need to challenge the guy, just realize that when a male is telling a good story he may get carried away. He may say he knocked somebody down when he only tapped the fellow, and he may say he had sex with a girl who just went for a walk hand-in-hand with him.

You may be tempted to tell a tall tale yourself sometime. If it is about sex with some girl everybody knows, hold off until the urge to lie passes. If you possibly can! Here's why: afterward, when you are by yourself, you will know you have been a big phony. You may have impressed somebody who doesn't realize that all the guys are lying, but you and God know you were a phony. And it will bother you.

About some real thing that passed between you and a girl: the more it was true, the more you are a great guy if you tell nobody. Just keep it between you and the girl. If you brag about it, in a day or two the girl will probably hear about what a big mouth you have. Do you really want to spoil your friendship with a girl who shared something with you? And her father or brother may hear about it, too. Are you looking for that kind of trouble?

If you tell lies for a moment of phony glory with some guys, it will in time come out that your big-shot image is phony. And for a lot of people, no matter what really great thing you may have done at some time, you will be best known as a fake.

Last of all, think of the misery it can cause a girl to hear what people are saying about her. Things that you put into circulation, false or true. Even if you are a real stud, you can be a gentleman about it.

THE UNINVITED ERECTION

One of life's hazards for the vigorous young male is the uninvited erection.

Boys talk about this problem. "Boy, did I

have a boner in Boyle's class!" Boyle is a teacher, of course.

Or it might be Kraft's class and the boy calls it a "hard-on."

If a boy sits down and deliberately thinks about undressing a well-imagined and well-endowed female, he is pretty sure he will get an erection. But when an erection comes all by itself, uninvited, it can be very mystifying and embarrassing.

The position he is in—the sluggish flow of blood into his lower torso, tight jeans, some vibration such as you get while riding a bus—may be the cause of the erection. It doesn't take much.

If it comes on a bus, the guy may find himself riding four stops past his home stop before getting up and walking to the exit.

If it comes in Boyle's class or Kraft's class, he hopes he won't be called on to go to the blackboard!

Sooner or later every male has to stand up with a big erection. From this he learns something. One, it probably goes down right away. Two, if it doesn't go down, people probably won't notice. The world is not full of crotch-watchers. Most people aren't hoping or expecting to see bulging pants. And when they do, they don't care much. If anyone does notice, it is just one of those things. Not a major disaster.

The mind can bring on an erection and it can make one go down. One male thinks of an icy shower or a pitcher of ice water poured on his penis. This works almost as well as the real thing. Another boy thinks of someone who is the opposite of sexually arousing. Boyle or Kraft, maybe. Or the principal. Or of something dismal like having a tooth drilled.

An erection can come when the male is near a girl. Dancing, or sitting with thighs touching. Or sitting and making out. If the girl notices, she may ignore it or she may disengage and say something ordinary like, "Hey! How are things in Boyle's class?" Or, "How's your cousin in Milwaukee?"

Sometimes after making out, but not having an orgasm or an ejaculation, after a strong, long-lasting erection, the boy's testicles may ache. They may turn that dark color that gives rise to the expression "blue balls." This will not harm him or his sexual equipment. The ache and the bluish color will go away.

When there is an erection there is usually a little oozing from the penis. This is some of that sperm-bearing seminal fluid that comes before the big ejaculation. And this is why pulling out before ejaculation, called *coitus interruptus,* is not a good contraceptive method at all.

MASTURBATION

Masturbation is a private act for most males. Thinking of having sex with a girl or woman, they usually close a fist around the shaft of the penis, after it is erect, and move the fist up and down as if it were the imaginary female's vagina. This produces stronger and stronger sensations in the penis until the ejaculation comes, along with the contractions in the groin and the most intensely pleasurable sensations known to man. Semen shoots out of the penis into the running water of the shower, into a tissue, or into some convenient receptacle. Masturbation relieves the sexual tension, the desire to have sex, for a short while. But it does not replace the desire to have sex with a real, live female.

All through the male's life, when he is without female companionship, he will probably return to the adolescent pleasure of masturbation. In fact, it is no longer regarded as particularly juvenile to masturbate. Men away from their wives are regarded as wise to masturbate instead of going to prostitutes and risking robbery and venereal disease. Masturbation is not known to have any bad effect on health or sanity.

It need not worry a boy to know that he masturbates now and then, more often, or even frequently, and it is also harmless if he stops for a period of months or years. Youths often do this, even before they begin to be sexually active with females. They become preoccupied with other things. When a male does not masturbate or have any other sexual outlet, he will probably have some wet dreams, which are also known as *nocturnal emissions*.

A young male will sometimes be masturbating and stop before finishing, or coming to orgasm. He should not worry about this. The fact is, outside thoughts sometimes interrupt sexual activity. This can happen even while having sex with a female. While masturbating this concerns only the boy, but when a man is making love to a woman he will want to see that she has her satisfaction even if he doesn't want to go on. He may bring her to orgasm with his hand or by some other means. Between lovers who have a good understanding, this is acceptable behavior.

In most families a youth is not teased or otherwise troubled about his private sexual behavior. Fathers and brothers don't pound on the bathroom door and yell coarse remarks. The dried semen that appears on sheets and pajama pants is not commented on. (It washes out easily, incidentally.) The wholesome attitude toward all this is that it is a sign of youth and health.

PREMATURE EJACULATION

A male who is about to have sex with a female may ejaculate, or "come," before he wants to do so. That is, before he has thrust and moved long enough after entering the female or even before he has entered. Ejaculating while fully clothed, during dancing or petting, is well known among the young. It is a sign of high enthusiasm and excitement that disappears as the male acquires sexual experience.

The erotic dream that a male has just before or during an involuntary emission is often more like premature ejaculation than like satisfactory sexual intercourse. Often the dreaming male is just about to enter the vagina when he ejaculates. Then he wakes up.

Some mature males have a habit of ejaculating prematurely when attempting intercourse. This behavior pattern is easily changed. A few consultations with a sex therapist will teach the man and his wife or lover to overcome this habit together.

While some erections end in premature ejaculation, some go down without any ejaculation at all. Every night, the average male in youth or the prime of life will have several erections while sleeping.

HOW OFTEN SHOULD I?

There is no rule about how often any male should have ejaculations, whether through intercourse, masturbation, or nocturnal emissions.

Back in the old days, when the older generation gave a lot of thought to stopping youths from masturbating because it was sincerely believed to be harmful, certain Spartan measures were supposed to discourage the practice. Cold showers daily, or more often, were recommended. A cold shower will indeed have a discouraging effect on an erection. Cold water makes the penis shrink to its smallest size. But the effect is not lasting. A quarter hour after a cold shower the youth can have another erection.

And it used to be believed that vigorous daily exercise would tire the youth out healthfully and keep his mind off sex. In fact, exercise makes a male more vigorous and sexier.

Almost all boys masturbate. It is no longer considered a health problem even by those who are still somewhat opposed to masturbation on moral grounds. Most religious leaders take a milder view of masturbation than they did a generation or two back. But if masturbation is not as vigorously opposed as it once was, it is still a private act. In the home it can be done without anyone ever interrupting the youth in the act if he is allowed the usual privacy of the bathroom or bedroom. Everyone should knock before entering either of these rooms—parents or children.

FRIENDLY OR LOVING INTERCOURSE

Good sex comes most often to a couple who have a private place, no fear of interruption, and complete peace of mind and willingness on both sides.

When we say "good sex" we mean sex that is enjoyable to both male and female partners. To serve its purpose as a way of starting a pregnancy, sex need not be enjoyable. But as a mutual pleasure and a way of achieving great closeness there should be time for the man to hug and kiss and caress the woman until she is aroused and partly on the way to orgasm before he inserts his penis into her vagina. She should be lubricated, or wet, inside her vagina, and she should want to have the man enter her. Most lovers agree not to have the man enter until she has given a signal for him to do so.

The length of time between insertion of the penis and ejaculation is something that a couple will agree on as they acquire experience with each other. A man who can control his ejaculations well is very likely to continue intercourse until the woman has had one or more orgasms, then to allow himself to have an orgasm and ejaculate. If the male "comes" before the female has had her orgasm, he can make sure that she is satisfied too, before disengaging from her. He may stroke or lick her clitoral area until she has an orgasm, or hold her in his arms while she masturbates. This is of course more loving and intimate than rolling away from her, leaving her to masturbate by herself.

The most satisfactory sex is generally agreed to be between people who have a sustained relationship—who have been together for some time and feel secure in each other's company. Casual sex, hastily agreed on between people who have just met or who have no real feeling for each other, is often a disappointing experience. Even when it is physically satisfactory, the lack of emotional closeness makes such sexual encounters rather sad.

LEARNING FROM AN OLDER WOMAN

You may hear someone say that the good old way to introduce a young man to sex was to take him to a kindhearted prostitute to be taught the ritual of intercourse. Or, even better, for him to have a relationship with an older woman who would personally undertake his sexual education. As a sexually inexperienced male, you may wonder if you have any chance of meeting such a prostitute or older woman.

On the whole, this is an idea to be used as a fantasy while masturbating, and not to try to arrange with a real prostitute or experienced woman.

A prostitute is usually not good-natured and is interested only in taking the man's money and making him ejaculate as speedily as possible so that she can take on the next customer. You are very likely to pick up a venereal disease from her instead of any very helpful tutoring in the art of love.

Older women willing to teach young men of 13 to 17 the ways of sex are not found in every neighborhood, and when they *are* found they are more likely to be mentally disturbed than good-hearted. Once a youth is involved with such a woman, she may be very hard to get loose from. She is apt to get drunk and phone the boy's home to have interesting chats with his mother. Her husband is also likely to want to talk to the boy or his family. It could turn into a real mess.

THE MEN WHO SEEK OUT TEENAGE BOYS

Every police officer in a town of any size has heard stories of the friendly grown men who start conversations with young teenage boys and then invite the boys to come with them somewhere more private. A ride on a motorcycle or in a nice car may be part of the bait. Men of this sort are arrested every week. And boys are being lured into sexual relationships with grown men. Boys may be kidnapped, sexually abused, and kept prisoner by threats and by the use of drugs. The drugs keep the boys slowed down mentally and confused and unable to escape.

There are men who like to get close to young boys, to handle their genitals, perhaps to have anal sex with them. They are very often pleasant-seeming men, not frightening at all unless you have been warned about being picked up by strangers.

You may have met someone like that and gone your own way after talking with him awhile. The best way is to say you are expected home shortly and leave politely. Men like this are interested in boys who are drifting around, not expected anywhere. The kid with a family that wants to know where he is can be more dangerous.

Every boy should know how these men behave and recognize them. You should understand that this is very likely to happen to you, because hardly a man can be found who doesn't have some memory of meeting one of these men during adolescence.

Here's how you are likely to meet a man like this. It will probably happen in a park, at a ball game, in a public library, or some other public place. You may have used the restroom when a nice-looking man speaks to you. He asks if you enjoyed the game or something like that.

He has a nice way of talking about things that are interesting to you. Probably he offers you a candy bar or a soda.

Do you have a girl friend? he wants to know. Do you go places with her? What do you do with her? He seems to take it for granted that you are into some kind of sex with some girl. The things he says about you make you feel like a big-shot who knows a thing or two. He'll feel your muscle and talk about what an athlete you must be. Maybe you know he's kidding you a little, but his line of talk makes you feel good, too.

He'll ask you questions about yourself and your interests, and make it easy for you to talk to him. And you may feel pretty grown up, talking like this with a grown guy. Sometime you'll have to come to his place and see some of his pictures and videotapes. You know he means porno tapes, and maybe you *would* like to see them.

If you go with this friendly guy, you may be in for real troubles and serious risks. What he is doing is illegal, and for you it can mean being picked up by the police. You can be pulled into a life of drug addiction and male prostitution. And your safety and your life may be at risk.

Since these men know they are doing something for which they can be arrested, they sometimes get panicky and want to get rid of the boy who can tell the police about them. This is one reason boys are murdered.

Another reason is that some of these men like to torture or kill boys as part of their sexual thrill. Some of these criminals have killed and buried many boys before being arrested.

It is very important to understand that these men don't look or act like monsters, or even like frightening men. Boys who go with them may see a chance to get nice clothes and other expensive things that they have never had—and just for doing something that is only like masturbating, after all.

Many boys who have been lured by men of this kind had never heard of any of the dangers involved. Now people are trying to get the information about these dangers to boys through the police, the schools, and television.

When you are out in public places, be polite to strangers but don't get into long talks with them. Always be on your way from one place to another, not lounging around as if nobody cares where you are. Avoid going into lonely areas by yourself. Be alert; play it safe.

Here's something else to avoid: offers of jobs from total strangers, or of deals where you will get something for helping out for a short time. You can be grabbed and kidnapped if you get near a car or truck. Stay away, stay back, say, "No, thanks!" and get away from there.

If you ever meet a man who behaves toward you as though he might be trying to get you off by yourself, be sure to report the happening to your family. *They* may decide to report it to the police, who may have had several such reports in your area. They may be looking for the man who tried to get friendly with you. Reporting him to the police may prevent harm or death to some other boy who is less alert than you are.

BOY BABY-SITTERS

If you ever take a job as a baby-sitter for small children, be very careful how you play with them, what kind of stories you tell them, and avoid doing anything that you don't want them to tell their parents about the next day.

A number of boy baby-sitters have gotten into trouble by behaving improperly with small children entrusted to their care. They have been seemingly nice boys, and the parents thought they were very trustworthy—but that turned out not to be so.

It frequently happens that children like the baby-sitter very much and like to play wildly and roughhouse with him; or they may hug and kiss him and show "big love" for this entertaining fellow who makes a real party out of baby-sitting them. A silly game with little children sometimes turns into something the baby-sitter wishes had never happened.

A boy who takes a job as a baby-sitter has to know that he has no intention of doing anything even remotely sexual with the children. And he has to avoid doing or saying anything that he would not want repeated or reported, even if it is really harmless.

Lots of boys make very reliable sitters. But every baby-sitter must understand the big responsibility that goes with the job, and must know exactly what he is *not* going to do as well as all the things the parents have asked him to do.

7

Dealing With Rape

Probably you have heard about rape on the television news or read about it in the newspaper. Or heard someone talking about it. Rape is a crime done by a man against another person, usually a girl or woman. The rapist forces his victim to have some kind of sex with him, using physical violence or threats to make her do it. The rape victim nowadays is encouraged to complain to the police and to help them to find and arrest the criminal by describing his appearance and behavior in detail, and to get help in recovering from all effects of the crime.

It is an ugly crime that causes pain and humiliation to the victim. If a girl or woman doesn't want to have sex, and is not doing it with someone she likes, who will make love to her and bring her to an accepting mood, with her sex organs ready, the penetration can be both painful and damaging. And very often harmful violence goes with the rape—beating, choking, and other kinds of hurting. This is done partly to overcome the woman, but with many rapists it is part of their sexual behavior to hurt and do harm. Lovers bring *love* to their sexual acts with other people; rapists bring anger and hate. Psychologists believe that the rapist is a man with a long grudge against women.

We don't know in every case what has turned a man into a rapist, but in his mind sex is connected with anger, violence, and revenge for things the rapist feels sure the world has done to him. He does not act purely out of a need for sexual relief. Most males who feel that they must have sex will try to approach a woman, or go to a prostitute, or they will masturbate. The idea of forcing brutally to get sex is not an ordinary male's idea.

We are not sure whether sexually exciting movies, shows, and magazines tend to make some men commit rape. Certainly a great many men who do read or look at pornography never commit rape.

Sometimes two or three or a whole gang of males will catch a girl in a lonely place and rape her, or kidnap her and take her somewhere to commit the crime.

In most of the rape cases reported in the news, the rapist is a stranger or someone the victim knows only slightly. He is to some extent mentally disturbed, or he may be drunk or under the influence of drugs. The rapist is not always able to carry out an act of sex. He may ejaculate too soon, or he may not be able to have an erection. But the violence and fear that come with rape also come with *attempted* rape.

Rapists often injure their victims severely or even kill them. The killing may not really be intended, but as the rapist beats or chokes his victim, making her cry and beg him to stop, he often goes too far and kills her. There is another reason why rapists kill their victims: to keep them from telling the police who did the crime, or to keep them from pointing out the rapist in a lineup of strangers in the police station.

AVOIDING RAPE SITUATIONS

Rape is known to happen most often in certain places, at certain times, and in certain situations. It is only sensible to avoid the rape situations, so we will offer here a number of things to avoid, to be cautious about, and never, never, never to do. These pieces of advice are not only for young girls, because rapists are famous for crimes against older women, even up into the nineties. Also against babies and children, and against boys.

Never hitchhike. You never know who will stop for you, or where he will take you. Harmless or friendly family people may pick you up, but you may end up in the morgue, victim of a rape-murder. Many, many hitchhikers have ended up just like that. So, no matter how many people you know who have gotten away with hitchhiking, no matter if you have done it yourself in the past, *don't hitchhike*. Don't hitchhike with another person, either. Pairs of young people have been raped, too.

If a stranger, or someone you don't know well, offers you a lift in his car, just say, "No, thanks," and keep going. No matter how nice he looks or how fabulous his car may be.

Avoid people who look weird or like bums. This may sound snobbish, but we don't care. Plenty of people who look degraded and weird *are* degraded and weird.

Avoid drunken men. Many men who have behaved decently when sober have become rapists when their mental processes got fogged by alcohol. Maybe drunks can't make love very well, but they can make a violent attempt at rape.

Never open the door when you are home alone and the bell rings. Find out who is there. Ask, "Who is it?" and don't open unless you know the name and the voice, and feel safe with that person. If a stranger is outside, just don't open up. If he says he has an emergency, tell him to try another house. Keep the door locked, and if the stranger won't go away, phone the police. You should always have police and emergency numbers right by the phone.

Never tell a strange phone caller that you are alone at home. If you answer the phone and the caller asks if your parents are home, say yes—but they are busy and can't come to the phone.

Never walk alone in the park. Nor on an old right-of-way or any other lonely path or trail. Take your stroll or hike in the daytime with a friend.

Never walk alone on dark streets, either in your neighborhood or downtown or anywhere else.

Avoid business buildings after office hours.

Avoid getting into elevators with only one person if the person gives you any kind of wrong impression. You probably won't be raped in the elevator, but a rapist might force you at knifepoint to get off on an empty floor.

Don't accept a storekeeper's invitation to go back into the storeroom to look at something. Say, "No, thanks—never mind." And leave the store.

Avoid staying late after school unless you are with a teacher or someone else you know. Rapists—both boys and grown men—have been known to hide in school buildings and wait for lonely girls or women.

WHEN SOMEONE YOU KNOW ACTS WEIRD

Rape is not always done by a stranger. Neighbors, bosses, schoolmates, and even relatives may begin to act weird and make you feel frightened. Pay attention to that feeling! If a man or boy is getting too familiar, getting too close, talking about sex or your body, get away quickly to a safe place. And tell your parents about it.

HOW DO YOU ACT WITH A RAPIST?

What do you do if you are raped, or if someone tries to rape you? In spite of all your caution, what could you do if it happened?

Do you struggle? Scream? Try to grab the knife or gun? Try to knee him in the testicles?

If you are free and can run, do it—and scream! Make all the noise you can. Don't try to act cool—make a hullabaloo. This has been known to frighten off men who were about to grab.

On the other hand, if you are grabbed, we have our doubts about your being able to fight off or struggle away from a male. You may only force him to use more brutal methods on you and get yourself badly hurt or killed.

But if you have been grabbed, there are things you might try to turn him off. Girls who have cried and humbly begged the attacker not to do it have been released. It seemed to satisfy the rapist's need to dominate a female. Or perhaps he wanted a woman who fought and had to be subdued violently.

Girls have been advised to try to be disgusting in some way, so that the rapist wanted nothing to do with them. You can say you are having your period, that you have gonorrhea or herpes or syphilis. Girls have urinated, let their bowels move, vomited—using signs of fear as protection. The rapist usually wants to be brutal to a nice, desirable female—not a disgusting slob. Why should you be a nice, desirable female for *him?* These are things some girls can do. You may not be able to, not even to save your life.

If rape is unavoidable, your aim should be to keep from being hurt unnecessarily. You can try going limp, making clear that you aren't going to fight it. You might say to yourself, "I'm not here, this isn't happening to *me.* Let's just relax so it doesn't hurt and he gets through with it." Oddly, this has sometimes made the rapist give up the attempt to commit rape. He wants to *force* himself on a female, not to be ignored by one.

Many rapists want most of all to force themselves on an unwilling female. A willing one turns them off. One way to get some rapists to quit is by saying, "Okay, but look—don't tell my boyfriend, okay? Just don't tell anyone, I don't want anyone to know I did this."

Maybe this speech won't make him stop, but when it is over you can beg him again not to tell. That reassures him that *you* aren't going to tell, and that there isn't any reason to kill you to shut you up.

WHAT TO DO AFTER RAPE

Get to a phone and call the police. They know everything that must be done for you immediately, and they will see that it is done.

First, you will be given medical treatment. You will get medication to prevent your contracting V.D. and to prevent your becoming pregnant.

Never walk alone in the park. Nor on an old right-of-way or any other lonely path or trail. Take your stroll or hike in the daytime with a friend.

Never walk alone on dark streets, either in your neighborhood or downtown or anywhere else.

Avoid business buildings after office hours.

Avoid getting into elevators with only one person if the person gives you any kind of wrong impression. You probably won't be raped in the elevator, but a rapist might force you at knifepoint to get off on an empty floor.

Don't accept a storekeeper's invitation to go back into the storeroom to look at something. Say, "No, thanks—never mind." And leave the store.

Avoid staying late after school unless you are with a teacher or someone else you know. Rapists—both boys and grown men—have been known to hide in school buildings and wait for lonely girls or women.

WHEN SOMEONE YOU KNOW ACTS WEIRD

Rape is not always done by a stranger. Neighbors, bosses, schoolmates, and even relatives may begin to act weird and make you feel frightened. Pay attention to that feeling! If a man or boy is getting too familiar, getting too close, talking about sex or your body, get away quickly to a safe place. And tell your parents about it.

they help you to understand that you can still love a man—that sex and rape are not the same thing, that a lover is someone who cares for you and is not another rapist. You will learn to understand that you have no reason to feel guilty. The sessions at the rape crisis center may last for several weeks, but they are worth the time spent on them. They will strengthen your thoughts and feelings about yourself and your future. In time you will be able to help other girls who have been raped.

As you are getting back to your normal self, your family should be helpful in every way. They will be taught to let you have your usual place in the household. You will do your usual chores and in no way will they treat you like a sick person. No one at home is to ask you questions about the rape—how it felt, et cetera. That is *out*. You have your professional counselors to help with that; for the rest of the world, no questions.

Your boyfriend must not ask questions about the rape, either. If he persists in talking about it, your friends at the crisis center will help you to deal with him. If he is sensitive and understanding, he will want to help you get over the experience. He *may* be one of those males who simply can't let go of the crazy idea that somehow you have been made less attractive. Some lovers can't accept rape as an accidental misfortune. If yours is one of these, you may have to face ending the relationship.

If rape ever happens to you, do get all

the help you are offered. Don't hide in your room. Use the help you need, that understanding people are ready to give you.

WHAT ABOUT BOYS AND RAPE?

Rape of males by males is a very common crime, especially in prisons. It happens outside of prisons, too, and therefore boys ought to read this chapter and make use of all the advice that is given about avoiding rape, avoiding the most serious injury the rapist may do, and getting necessary help after the rape.

Rape of males by females is something that we hear about once in a while. There are people who say it can't be done, but obviously a woman can force sex on an unwilling man. She can get him to have an erection even if he may not have wanted it at first, and she can force other humiliating actions on him. Fortunately, very few women are driven to do this kind of thing.

RAPE BY PERSONS KNOWN TO YOU

Male or female, you can be raped by men who are not strangers to you. It makes for a very complicated problem if you are raped by your sister's husband, for instance. You may not want to hurt your sister by reporting the rape; you may be afraid that the whole family will decide it must have been your fault. In cases like this, you should get to the school nurse for counseling and advice on how to get protection and help.

There is another kind of rape that is done by men who are known to the victim. In a number of states there is a crime on the books known as statutory rape. This is not rape in the sense of being violent or unwelcome to the victim; in fact, she may be in love with the guy. But if she is too young to give consent to the act of sex according to state law, anyone who has sex with her can be charged with statutory rape. This is something to bear in mind if you are the underage girl or the male thinking of having sex with her.

In your state, can you be charged with statutory rape for having sex with your present girl friend? If you are the girl, do you want to get your sweetheart into this kind of danger?

BEING MORE ALERT THAN FRIGHTENED

What you have read in this chapter may leave you scared. You may feel glad that Mom and Dad are in the house right now. In a little while you will feel brave again, but we hope you won't forget this advice about avoiding rape and how people deal with rape if it touches their lives.

Rape is an accident and most people get through life untouched by it. Like the person who is hit by lightning, the rape victim is not to blame. But you can follow the rules for avoiding lightning (don't swim in a thunderstorm, don't stand under a lonely tree on a plain), and you can follow the rules for avoiding rape.

Most people are never going to be rape victims, and you are probably not going to be one. But if you are sensible you will avoid the rape situations.

Most of the people you meet are never going to be rapists, either. Many grown-ups like to speak to young people, calling out "Hi, honeybunch!" to girls and "Hi, champ!" to boys. Or something like that. It only means that they are in a good mood. But you have no way of telling who the good guys and who the wrong ones are, so don't let any stranger do more than greet you. You can say "Hi" back if you want to, or you can ignore the greeting as if you didn't hear it or didn't think it was for you. But keep going. Don't have a conversation.

If people stop a car and ask directions, the simplest thing is to say, "I don't know," and let them drive on until they find a grown-up to ask. That isn't being a good Scout, but we say it is good sense, especially if you are young and small or *look* young and small.

If you are older-looking you may feel silly following "kids' rules" and avoiding strangers, but you still have to use your head. Grown-ups who deal with strangers all the time have to use *their* heads while traveling and on the job. Store-keepers do, repairmen who go into strange neighborhoods do, and even policemen follow rules in dealing with strangers. So, the more you use *your* head, the more you are acting like an experienced grown-up person.

8

Sharing With Your Parents

It's really great luck to have parents whom you can talk to. Who listen to you, and help you out with things when you want to be helped and still know how to let you try some things out by yourself, and make your own mistakes if you have to. But you may not think that your parents are really like that. Maybe you feel that your parents are good parents but hard to talk to. There are plenty of things you would rather not discuss with them because all they do is get uptight and hassle you. Or you may think that when they talk to you they treat you like a baby. They won't talk straight with you, but always end up shaking a finger and telling you exactly how you should act in every situation. If you have a problem with a teacher, they say, "You go right up to him and say...."—and they say something then that would only make the teacher laugh at you, you think. You would rather use your own words.

It may be true that you have some kind of trouble talking with your folks and sharing with them your problems and your triumphs. But for your own sake you should feel free to talk to your parents, because you and your parents will enjoy these growing-up years more if things are friendly and open between you. Then, when the time comes that you really want to ask them for something important, it will be much easier to start that big discussion—and easier to carry it through to the end. You may have a real problem and then you will want to get them on your side right away. Or you may just be bothered about something and want to hear what a grown-up has to say about it. So it is good for you to be able to talk to your parents. And they will like it. Parents get to feeling lonely and shut out, with one of these Silent Sam teenagers in the house. Have a heart! Say something to Mom or Dad! Share something with them today!

Perhaps this suggestion astounds you. You never thought that perhaps your parents would like you to make some kind of friendly gesture. And as for sharing some experience with them—ha! Because so many experiences just can't be shared with them. They are the *last* people you'd tell.

In a typical teenage day, you may say, the big things just can't be shared. For instance: at 9:00 A.M. you went into Boyle's class without having done the homework. You felt so dumb! Especially because Boyle is the most sarcastic teacher in school, and was just waiting to catch you like that. What a rotten hour that was! And you aren't going to share it with your parents. It was bad enough sharing it with Boyle.

At lunch you sat with friends in the lunchroom and they talked a lot of French they just learned and you don't take French, so you felt shut out and very, very jealous. And you felt ashamed of feeling jealous; you can hardly share that with *yourself*. And you definitely won't share it with the folks.

In Kraft's class you had a daydream about "doing it" with guess who, Kraft. Kraft is pretty foxy for a teacher. While you were daydreaming she spoke to you several times before you came to and heard her. She wanted you to come pick up a composition off her desk, but you had such an erection you couldn't. Then you jumped up and ran to get it bent over like Groucho Marx, and everybody laughed. You were ashamed to clown around like that in her class because she thinks you are intelligent—or did until today. Your parents would not like to hear about that.

All right, you can't share *everything*. But we still say that you will enjoy life more if only you make yourself share a little more with your parents. And the question now is *what*? What can a teenager share with parents?

Glad you asked!

SHARING WORRIES ABOUT SEX

You can ask more of these questions about sex when you are with your parents. That would be an important concern to share with them.

This is a central issue in your life, and you never share it with them. Why? Because years ago you asked them a certain question and they told you the stork brought you. And after that you asked them how your sister got *out* of Mommy's stomach, and they wouldn't tell you. And every time you asked them they were no help. They have always been the kind of parents who can't talk to their kids about sex.

So how can you ask them anything about sex now?

Simple. You are older now. You are more like a grown person. They would be less embarrassed talking about it to you now. Things have changed.

But, you feel, you have already learned so much about sex, and now the subject has gone beyond where did Sis come from, and *you* are the embarrassed one, because sex is so close to *you*.

Still, there are a lot of fine points that they can help you with. They may be sort of old-fashioned, but they want to help, and if you let them know more of your problems they could help with things that aren't in sex-ed class or that great sex book for young teens.

FOR INSTANCE, WHO BUYS THE BROWNIES?

There is a big issue that you could take up with them. You were at the dance in the gym.

You danced with a girl (when it was a square dance, because you can *do* that) and then they opened the refreshment table with the cider and the brownies and you wanted to impress the girl and get the cookies but you had never bought a girl refreshments. Would that be okay, or too male chauvinist pig? What happened was that you asked her if she wanted any refreshments and she said no, and you wanted some but you felt funny buying cider and a brownie just for yourself, so instead neither of you had anything and you both got tongue-tied. And you think she really wanted some but didn't feel right about saying so. So what about all that?

Now that is the kind of thing parents can help you thrash out, even if they were a little uptight about where you came from eleven years ago.

HOW DO YOU ASK HER THAT?

After the dance, everybody who lives in the neighborhood of the school and wasn't being driven home began walking home, and you wanted to walk her to her house but two of her girl friends were standing there, and they lived near her, so how could you suggest that she walk just with you when she always walks with them?

You ended up walking in their direction with all three and they kept asking why you weren't walking toward *your* house.

If you felt like discussing things like that, your parents would be pleased to talk it all over with you and give advice on how to single a girl out.

WHAT DO YOU TALK ABOUT?

If you were to take this girl out, you know you would freeze up when it came to talking to her. Maybe you can talk to her all right in school, during the day, but out on a date it would be different. And your parents could explain how you get the other person talking about what interests her, and that will make her very happy to be talking and not tongue-tied and she would be doing all the work.

AND WHAT DO YOU DO WHEN NOBODY'S TALKING?

You are at a party at somebody's house and you have tried this idea of getting her to talk about something she is interested in, and you know she has been to Ireland four times so you ask her about that and she is talking a blue streak. So that was fine, but nobody else at the party was talking, they were all necking with the lights low, and you and she were standing and talking and it got more and more embarrassing, and the more it was embarrassing the more she talked. That was how she tried to avoid noticing what everyone was doing, because she was nervous about it. And the next day a guy said you were a nerd, standing talking to that girl when everybody else was making out. Now your parents could tell you how they feel about a party where parents let the kids neck and how they understand that you and this girl were feeling funny and what you could do if that ever came up again.

When you talk to your parents about that, it turns out that they really know a lot about how you and the girl feel when you like each other but don't want to sit in the same room with everybody else making out. You would like to kiss her but not like that and not there. And your parents know what you are talking about and they back you up and they tell you how to leave a party like that, when you have gone in somebody else's car and he doesn't want to leave yet. So your move is to phone home to see if Dad will come for you, which he usually will. And for a backup plan, you have this five dollars you don't spend but just keep to pay for a cab if you get stuck somewhere like that again. And Dad will give you the five to keep just for that.

Then Mom tells you about mad money, and how when she was very young a girl always had mad money for paying cab fare when she had to leave the guy she came with because he was starting to pressure her into something she didn't want to do. And the three of you laugh and they tell you a lot of things to say or do in embarrassing situations.

MY PARENTS TALK TO ME ABOUT THAT

In a while you find you and your parents are getting to be very talkative and they will answer questions about almost anything, like: why the girl who lives on the corner gave up her baby for adoption when her family was rich enough to keep it. And why that block is full of teenage prostitutes. And why some men pay boy prostitutes to go up to their hotel rooms. And why the school doesn't fire the gym teacher although the gym teacher seems to be homosexual. And one by one they tell you all sorts of things you thought they wouldn't talk about, because now you are older and they are less embarrassed.

One day in school the guys in the cafeteria are talking about the gym teacher and wondering why the school doesn't fire him, and you explain that he is good at his job, and anyway, nowadays people are careful how they fire minority people who have strong legal protection from their organizations. And the guys ask how you know all that and you say, "My folks and I were talking about it." And the guys' eyes get round because they didn't know you could talk about that with your folks.

SO YOU TELL YOUR DAD THAT

So you tell your dad that, about how your friends were impressed that you could talk to your parents about things like that. And your dad says, "We are kind of old-fashioned people, but just for that reason I want you always to feel you can talk to us. Whatever it is, try talking to Mom or me about it. We've talked a lot about things that bother you and about kids who are in trouble, and you see that Mom and I aren't hard to talk to. So this is what I want you to know: if you ever get in a jam, you can talk to me. Okay? Now I know you are a sensible kid, but anybody could make a mistake. And if you do, I don't want you running away and getting into trouble. You can always talk to me, whatever it is that is bothering you."

That is sort of scary, knowing that Dad thinks you might get into trouble. But it feels good to know that he wants to be the first to hear if you are ever in some kind of fix like that.

You've come a long way with your parents since you thought they were too uptight ever to talk to you about your concerns. And it all started when you asked them about buying a girl some brownies and cider.

It seems they were dying to talk to you but you just weren't talking to them.

And one night you are talking to your Dad and suddenly you are telling about the time you had an erection in Kraft's class, the whole thing. And then you feel funny, like maybe that particular story is a little too much for Dad. And he sits there looking at you without saying anything for a while and you begin to feel uptight.

And then Dad says, "Did you ever get straightened out with that homework for Mr. Boyle?"

And you see he was more worried about your falling behind in your schoolwork than about a silly thing like why you had to lean over Kraft's desk that day.

A FINAL WORD FOR THE REAL YOU

The episodes we have just told about are very lifelike, from our experience. But we know that you are not really the kid who has teachers named Boyle and Kraft and had to go without the cider and brownies. And your real parents are not just like that kid's. But we hope you got some ideas from all that about beginning to share more things with your parents. Maybe you can't share everything. But maybe you should share more than you do. And you really ought to have in your mind the idea that your parents are there to help, and unless you share with them they *can't* help. Okay?

9

Knowing When To Ask For Help

Grown-up is a wonderful way to feel, and one of the things that goes with it is not asking for things all the time but knowing what is yours to take and taking it. Asking for help all the time goes with babyishness and not knowing how to tie the laces on your shoes! Or how to cut your own meat. You don't like to ask for help at all if you can avoid it, now that you're really pretty grown-up, taking driver's ed, maybe, and helping a friend with some work on his car. Having a part-time job, friends all over town, liking people to know you are pretty self-reliant.

You know how to handle more and more things and your self-confidence grows and grows. And more and more you have the knack of talking to grown-ups like a grown-up, and getting grown-up answers.

If something about life is still unknown to you, and it seems to be turning into a nagging worry, you think, "I've got to find out more about that." The next time you are in the library you try to find a book about the thing that you're wondering about. That may be how you got *this* book.

There are some problems that come up in life that call for more than an intelligent interest, however. They call for *action*, and usually it has to be action of an expert kind. This kind of emergency can't be handled by doing it yourself. You need help, and you need it right away. The grown-up thing to do in these emergencies is to ask for that help as soon as you can, before the emergency is out of control.

You know it's right to call the fire department if there is a fire, and the police department if there is a crime or an accident. You don't wonder about that, but grab the phone and dial the right number. There are other emergencies that need immediate help that are less well known, and we want you to know about them and to know how to get help right away.

YOUR FRIEND HAS V.D.

Let's say that *you* have been too smart to get V.D., because you know that the only way to get V.D. is by sexual contact with a person who has it, and you have avoided that. If you have avoided all sexual contact with everybody—what can we

say? You just haven't gotten V.D. Congratulations—
on being smart, and on not having V.D.!

Or you don't have V.D. because you have
had sex only with someone who has sex only
with you. Neither has ever had sex with anyone
else, so V.D. hasn't had the slightest chance of
getting into your tight little partnership. You
have been smart, because you have stayed with
somebody you feel you can trust, and you have
been lucky because that person really has been
trustworthy. That makes you partly smart and
partly lucky—congratulations on both!

Or you are just lucky because no signs of
V.D. have shown up yet, although you have had
sex with a person, who is not really a one-
person person, but has had sex with a number
of friendly characters. Well—congratulations on
being lucky, maybe. We say *maybe* because maybe
you *do* have V.D., only the symptoms haven't
shown up yet. If you were a grown-up, and
smart, do you know what you would do? You
would go to a doctor or to a clinic to be tested
for V.D. Because you wouldn't want to wait for
the obvious symptoms, like sores or liquid oozing from your genitals.

But your friend—ah, your poor friend hasn't
been so lucky. Your friend has gone and caught
a case of V.D. and now he is up the creek. He is
looking at his penis every time he gets a chance,
to make sure it isn't all a bad dream. He keeps
hoping it's just a food-allergy rash or a pimple
or poison ivy—but he is afraid it is V.D. He
doesn't dare ask for help, because he knows he
is going to be yelled at. They will ask him where

he got it, and a lot of people will be mad at him for telling on them. Finally he tells *you* because he has to tell *someone*. What can *you* tell *him*?

We have been talking about a male friend who has caught V.D., but all this is just as true for a girl, so keep that in mind.

Here's what you should tell your friend. First, he has an illness. An illness that doesn't get better by itself, like a cold or a stubbed toe. He's *got* to get medical treatment from a doctor. He should tell his parents, too.

Okay—they're going to hit the ceiling! Let's be realistic and assume that. There are some very intelligent and loving parents who always want to be *told*, no matter what the bad news is. But even so, we must allow them to blow off some steam, to show some anger! Or tears. There is no use expecting them to be supercool and only say, "Claude, we're very glad you have told us that you have V.D. instead of being foolish and trying to hide it. It shows that you trust us, and we are proud of your trust in us."

Let us count on his parents' being normal and giving him hell—for a *while*. But there will be a limit to the hard time they give him, and then they will begin helping him to get treatment. If they have a family doctor, they will send him to the doctor; if they get their medical help from a clinic, they will go there with him. In either case, he will get the treatment he needs. And the V.D. will be cured.

If he doesn't go through the blowup with his parents and get the treatment, his health may be harmed for life—very seriously. You don't fool around with V.D.—you get it cured!

"But what if I tell my folks and they find out about everything, and Peggy's folks find out and want to kill her and me—and it isn't even V.D.?" your friend asks. "Then I have all that grief, and Peggy has all that grief, and it's all because I got scared and told my folks."

What can you say to that? Fortunately, there is an answer. He has to make sure it isn't V.D., and he has to tell his folks. So he'll get all the blowup and then they'll send him to the doctor. Only in this case the whole situation is a little better, because he doesn't have the infection.

"Listen," your friend may say. "If you were in this mess instead of me, do you swear that you would do what you're telling me to do?"

"Sure."

"No, don't just say sure—*swear*. Put up your hand and say you swear that if you're ever in this fix you will go and tell your folks."

"If I am ever in a fix where I think I may have V.D. I will tell my folks and get help."

That's the way to talk. And if you ever have the bad luck to get into that situation, *do* tell your parents. Not just because you swore, but because it is the one smart thing to do.

Let's suppose your friend—no, he's been through enough. Let's say it's *you* this time. Sure, you're too smart to get yourself into this kind of trouble, but just *suppose* you did, somehow or other. Let's suppose you are worried about possibly having V.D., for whatever reason. Maybe you have a sore or a discharge from your penis, or *something*. Or you have a good idea that you have been exposed to V.D.—you have had sex with someone who is promiscuous, who has sex with a lot of people. And you just can't get up the courage to face your parents.

You know you want to get treatment as soon as possible, if you do have V.D. And it may take you weeks to get up courage to tell Mom and Pop. Go tell someone else, and let that person be the first to break the news, and let him or her ask your parents not to come down on you too hard, because after all you feel bad enough already. And you have done the right thing by asking for help. Who would this person be? Maybe an uncle who has always been sympathetic. Maybe a grown sister or brother. A priest, rabbi, or minister. The school nurse. A doctor. Someone at the clinic.

Maybe you feel pretty sure that someone at home will lose control and beat you badly when the news breaks. In that case, tell the nurse or doctor or clinic person about your fear, and your folks will be warned against doing any violence to you.

In the preceding chapter we talked about the importance of talking to parents and sharing with them. Maybe the parents should be the ones to keep communications open, but it is your responsibility, too. Remember, a person who talks with you regularly about your problems is more likely to be on your side when you are in trouble.

In every young person's life there should be somebody who says, "If you are ever worried or in a jam, come tell me. No matter what it is. I'll want to know, and I'll do everything I can to help." When you are a parent, be sure you tell that to *your* child or children. Right now, as a person who is underage and has to count on parents for help, you just have to assume that your parents will help you when you really need help. Unless you know that your parents really are dangerous or untrustworthy, you have to assume that they will meet their responsibilities.

If, perhaps, one of your friends should have some good reasons why he or she feels that they have absolutely no one they can trust to talk with, they should be aware that in most states, now, a minor has the right to medical treatment for veneral disease without parental consent.

AIDS—WHY WE HAVE TO LEARN ABOUT IT

We have heard a lot of talk lately about a new disease called AIDS. In some ways, it is like a venereal disease, only much worse, because if you get AIDS, there is no cure. And, the saddest part is that most people who have gotten AIDS in the past have died from it. Although we can't cure AIDS right now, we do know many things about how someone can get AIDS. Like so many other problems we have talked about in this book, when you have some knowledge about how you may be harmed by certain things, like the ways some people may approach you to have sex with them, you can help protect yourself from some of the dangers. Also, it is important to know more about AIDS so that you are *not* frightened into thinking that you may catch it when this is not likely to happen. Sometimes, fear, when it is caused by misinformation, can make us cruel to other people because we are afraid that they will hurt us in some way. Unfortunately, because AIDS is a frightening disease some people are afraid to even shake hands with a person who has AIDS, or, if a child had AIDS because of a blood transfusion—that was before we became more careful about blood used in transfusions—there were some parents who did not want this child to be in the same classroom as their own children. We can understand their feelings but such fear is not based on what we know about how someone can get AIDS.

The letters in AIDS stand for Acquired Immune Deficiency Syndrome. What this long name means is that if a person has AIDS, then that part of the body known as the *immune system* is not able to fight off, with its own natural means, some diseases which have been associated with AIDS. These diseases may cause a variety of serious infections which spread through the body because the *immune system*, which has become damaged, can no longer help protect that person. Sometimes, cancers develop which might not have developed if the immune system had not been weakened by AIDS.

Can we prevent AIDS with a vaccine, like we prevent measles? Unfortunately, just as we have no cure at the present time, we have no vaccine to prevent it with. For now, all we can suggest to you is to follow the advice of the medical authorities so that you are not likely to get the disease. However, as serious as the disease of AIDS is, most physicians and researchers in the medical field that we have read and talked with tell us that a person is not likely to get it if they follow some commonsense precautions. But, in order to know how to protect yourself, without becoming overly fearful and suspicious of people who have AIDS, you have to know how it is that one person can get this disease from another.

For the most part, it is through *sexual contact* that you are most likely to get AIDS. But you can't get AIDS from just anybody, and only certain kinds of sexual contact is what is considered to be high risk. Some people mistakenly think that only homosexuals can get AIDS, or that all homosexuals have AIDS. Neither of these statements are true. Although AIDS first came to public attention because it was showing up in large numbers among sexually active homosexual men, it was not because they were homosexuals, but that the kind of sex some of these men were having was the kind by which the AIDS virus is most easily passed. What kind of sex are we talking about? And, what are the other ways that AIDS can be transmitted from one person to another?

As we said, the most common way is through

sexual contact with someone—it could be either a heterosexual *or* a homosexual—who has the AIDS virus in his or her body. Most authorities say that it is passed from one person to another when they are in intimate sexual contact, that is, when the man's penis is placed inside the woman's vagina, or they are engaging in fellatio or cunnilingus. In all these methods, since some fluid is passed from one person to another, the AIDS virus may be passed too, if one of the persons has it. There are other ways in which fluid may be passed from one person to another, for example, during anal intercourse. That is when the penis of the man is put inside the anus of the woman. Since it is so easy to break the skin inside the anus this way, the AIDS virus, if it is present, can easily pass from one person to another. Because this is the way many male homosexuals engage in sex, researchers believe that this is why the disease spread so rapidly among male homosexuals. So you can see that this is not a *homosexual* disease but that some kinds of sex make it easier to catch AIDS.

What about prevention during vaginal or sexual intercourse? If you do not have sex, that's one way to prevent it. If you do, then it appears that the most sensible precaution is to use a condom in order to prevent the passing of fluids from one person to another. Will this guarantee that you cannot get AIDS? Of course not! We can never be 100 percent sure as long as two people engage in sexually intimate contact, but it is better to take *some* precautions than none at all.

What about deep kissing (french kissing), or being bitten by another person (in a playful manner, of course)? We cannot be sure, at this time, but most doctors and researchers do not think that it is likely that AIDS can be passed in this way, but even they are not positive, so use your common sense. Can petting, touching or casual kissing cause a problem? Again, you have to use your common sense. If you have an open wound and permit the body fluids of a strangers sexual organs to come into contact with it, this would not be wise. We know that it is difficult, when you are young, to stay with only one person when you are trying to learn about the opposite sex, but the more casual sex you have, with different partners, the greater the danger. Do not confuse casual sex with casual contact. When you hear people on the television or radio say that casual contact with a person who has AIDS is not likely to cause a problem, they are talking about such things as using the same eating utensils or shaking hands with them or simple kissing on the cheek, etc. When you hear people talking about casual sex, they usually mean intimate sex with a person that you don't know very well. That's not a smart thing to do.

Another way of getting AIDS would be to use a hypodermic needle to inject illegal drugs, or even medication, into your body after someone else who had AIDS used the needle himself. In a doctor's office, you would always get a new or sterilized needle but we know that drug addicts have a higher rate of AIDS than many other people because they often share their needle with other addicts, some of whom have AIDS.

Other ways of getting AIDS would probably not be of much concern to you but you should know about them. One would be to get the AIDS virus when you have a blood transfusion. But today, the blood banks are very careful about who they get blood from. The other known way is to be born from a mother who has AIDS while pregnant.

In short, we don't want to frighten you so that you will not want to be in the same room as a person who has AIDS, but when it comes to having sex, you must use your good judgment and be as prudent as possible.

WHAT HAPPENS IF YOU DO HAVE V.D.?

Suppose you do have V.D., and you have had the tests and the doctor or the clinic people are sure. You won't have to go into the hospital. You will be given medication and you will have to go back to the doctor or clinic for regular checkups until the infection is definitely cleared up.

You will be asked who gave you the V.D., and the only thing to do is to be truthful. This questioning is for the good of that person, who needs medical treatment as much as you do. And they will ask you the names of all the people you have had sex with, in case there has been more than one. All those people must be told that they have been exposed to an infectious disease. It is only fair to them. None of these people will be punished by the authorities. They will be treated as people who need medical treatment.

When you report that you think you may have V.D., you are not only doing the right thing for yourself—you are doing the right thing for the health of the community. And that is also true when you give the authorities the names of people with whom you have had sexual contact. You are helping the doctors and health authorities to keep the disease from spreading.

SUPPOSE YOU THINK YOU'RE PREGNANT?

Boys can read this part too, because part of it will be about the boy who made the girl pregnant.

You're the girl, let us say, who has a hunch that she may be pregnant. You have had sex and your period is late. Maybe you feel queasy and food is not interesting to you.

Maybe you think of telling the boy you had sex with—but cancel that idea. And maybe you will tell a girl friend while getting up your courage to tell Mom. Do that if you must, but remember that fewer people will get to know of your trouble if only your mother knows than if you tell a girl friend. That is a pretty reliable rule. As soon as you can, but picking a time when the two of you can be alone, tell your mother. That will give her a chance to have a bit of a fit if she needs to, before calming down and being helpful. The first thing to do is to get you to a doctor, clinic, family-planning center, or nearby hospital for an examination.

If you are pregnant, the doctor will not ask questions about the boy you have been having sex with. His interest will be in your health and in that of the baby that is now growing inside your body.

You will be told about caring for yourself, eating the proper food, being clean, having enough exercise, and preparing your body for what is coming, up to the time of the baby's birth.

You will be told about how long the baby has been growing inside you, and whether your body is now in its best condition. You could be examined to see if your body is right for a normal, vaginal birth. But, sometimes it may be necessary to have an operation called a cesarean section. This means that a surgical incision is made in the walls of the abdomen and uterus for the delivery of the baby.

This is what medical help provides. It does not suggest to you at first what choices you and your family ought to be looking at.

But there are choices that need to be examined very carefully. In such a situation, we do suggest that family members reach outside the family for help and advice.

You and your parents may know a clergyman whom you admire and who has been a friend. This is a person who can help you all see what needs to be considered in the light of your religious beliefs.

This is important when you and your family have been living with certain religious beliefs and points of view. You may have slipped from those beliefs in becoming pregnant, but if your religion means anything to you, you should look for counsel from that source.

You may find other help from some of the social agencies in your community. Counselors will talk with you and your parents about your options and what to expect. Such men and women usually do not take religious beliefs into account, but they will help you to face this problem in other ways.

We haven't said anything so far about the father of the baby you are carrying inside your body. The father may be a teenager like you. We've seen many such situations and the boy is usually not able to take any responsibility.

How could he help you during the time of your pregnancy? With comfort? With money? With trips to visit the doctor? With some kind of parenting when the baby is born?

If you are the boy in this case, your family should be told about the matter, and they, too, should be involved in getting the help you need. If you look for help from a member of your religious faith, or from a social worker, that is certainly a way of sharing the responsibility.

But for the mother-to-be, looking for help is the job of her parents and herself, with the boy's family or without them.

We suggest that another place to look for alternatives is in a clinic for women, or in an organization that gives information on birth control and also on good care for pregnant women and girls.

It is also helpful if your doctor, once you know the facts of your pregnancy, will discuss with you the options for a pregnant young teenager.

Even though we cannot deal with individual cases here, we can point out some of the questions to consider.

Should you have the baby?

If you do, should you raise it or put it up for adoption?

Should your parents raise your baby for you?

If you all agree that you should not have the baby, what are the facts about abortion? Where? When? How much does it cost?

How can you be helped to have a happy, normal life after you have had this experience?

All these and more are the questions that you and your family will need help with.

What about the boy (or the man) in this case? If you are the teenage boy and your girl friend tells you that you and she have started a baby, you do have a share in the problems. Of course, you cannot manage without *your* parents knowing and helping.

We are sure there will always be comments made by parents about "whose fault" it was. Such comments don't matter much and they certainly don't help. If you and your family want to show your maturity and your responsibility, then there is a loving kindness you can show to your girl. If possible, expenses should be shared, and you can be involved in the discussions about options.

We are not able to say what the final decisions should be and what your part should be in them. Since you are both teenagers, we hope you will find that the adults in your families will want to reach those decisions with the help we have mentioned, and with plenty of consideration for your feelings.

We are very sure that with such help—from a clergyman, a good counselor, a social worker, maybe a lawyer—the right decisions can be reached. In the best interests of your girl and you and the baby that you both started.

INCEST

When you have become involved in incest—sexual activities with someone in your family—you definitely need help. You cannot deal by yourself with the father who tries to become intimate with you, or with the older brother or sister who gets closer to you sexually than you like.

Cases of incest have many causes. We're not sure what all of them are. But we believe that an adult male who becomes interested in having sex with a young teenage girl may lack confidence in himself. He may feel inadequate when it comes to relationships with women nearer his own age. He may have had some unpleasant or unhappy experiences with one or more.

A teenage male in the family who tries to

have sex with a sister may be very curious and want to satisfy his curiosity in the "safety" of his own home. The family member who "started" the incest needs help, too. Incest is a bad thing for him to get involved in, too.

Whatever the reasons, as the girl, *it's not your fault.* And it's not your job to be a sexual companion for your father, stepfather, uncle, or older brother. If any of these attempts sex with a young girl in the family, he is guilty of a criminal act. If you are the victim, or if anyone tries to make you the victim, you must get help quickly.

Your mother *should* be your first stop for talking about what is going on. Sometimes a mother can't believe what you describe.

But if you are sure of your facts, or if she can be shown what is taking place, then she must act to protect you. In some family situations a word from the mother to the man or boy who is attempting incest will be enough. If that is not enough, then you and your mother must consult your most confidential adviser, such as your doctor or clergyman.

We hesitate to suggest bringing in the police. An incest problem may be solved without that. If you and your family get counsel from a clergyman or a social worker and the problem is stopped, we feel that you have done enough. But if the offender tries again to have sex with you, then it is *not,* and you do have to report the matter to the police.

A boy in a case of incest may be involved with a sister or an older woman. Or a male relative may attempt homosexual activities with the boy. In either case, the boy cannot let this go on. The activities are harmful to him and they are against the law. The boy is a victim of abuse, and the damage to him may change his whole life.

Many young victims of incest say nothing to anyone, but spend many years under a burden of guilt. They may feel that they are to blame in the business. That they invited the incest. They may want to protect an adult.

The underage victim of incest often feels that she is responsible for what has happened. She may feel sure that she "started it." But no one can hold this young victim responsible; it is the responsibility of the older person to avoid incest, and the law holds the older person responsible. To overcome mistaken feelings of guilt, the victim may need professional counseling or therapy at a clinic or social agency.

CHILD ABUSE

If you get a lot of physical punishment at home, beating with a fist, stick, or strap, or something as dangerous, you must go for help to the school nurse or the police. This is child abuse.

The chances are you will have marks of mistreatment and that you will need medical care, which will be provided.

It makes no difference who is abusing you, nor for what reason. There is no reason that excuses this treatment. You cannot be bad enough to deserve this, so don't feel that you deserve this treatment.

Young teenagers have been scarred and crippled for life from abuse such as this. Such abusers—mother, father, stepparent—may be convinced that they are trying to cure you of bad habits or evil ways. They may even have *you* convinced of this. But physical abuse is not good for you, and it is a punishable crime. If you or another child in your family is injured or abused, you must get help. Maybe you are not a perfect person, but no one has the right to injure you—not even your family.

Where do you go for help? Your mother—if she can help, and if she is not the one who is hurting you. But probably you will have to go outside the household where you live. Have you an older brother or sister who lives away from home? Or any other relative not living with you? Such a relative might help, if you showed him or her your injuries. They could talk to those who are abusing you, and that might make a change in the way you are treated.

If there is no improvement from within the family, go to the school nurse. She will look at your injuries and consult the police. The police can put a stop to the abuse, and they can see that you get medical treatment—with or without your family's okay.

MENTAL ABUSE

This is something that is very hard to prove, since there are no physical marks on the young person's body. And very often the victim describes treatment that almost every youngster gets at some time or another. You may feel that you are yelled at too much, made to feel worthless, not allowed any privileges, grounded too often and for too long. The treatment may be unfair, but it isn't really brutal.

If you feel that you are getting mental abuse from your parents, you should first try talking with them about what you must do to get better treatment. Get from them a list of things that they want you to stop doing, such as leaving the house without saying where you will be, slamming doors, picking your nose, leaving your stuff all over the house, slipping away without clearing the table, being on the phone for hours. And a list of things they want you to do—clear the table, make your bed, keep the grass trimmed and the walks swept, et cetera. Maybe both sides can come to a better agreement. You may understand better what they want; they may see that you are trying to improve your standing in the family. You should try this, anyway.

If your people are very unreasonable in their demands, and if you get very unusual treatment that can be called cruel even if it isn't physically damaging, collect a list of these things and see the school nurse. That is, if things happen to you such as being locked in a dark closet every day, being given something awful to eat, or anything that you find either frightening or disgusting. If the nurse thinks you are being treated in some unusually mean way, she may invite your parents to come and have a talk with her or with a counselor. Your parents may not realize that their behavior is generally considered peculiar.

Perhaps you may find a way to join some youth group where you can be treated in a more ordinary way, and be rewarded for your behavior instead of being always put down. That would make some of your life better, at any rate.

Any form of child abuse—physical or mental—is often a sign that the grown-up involved in it is having some serious problems. Parents have marriage problems, job problems, and problems with mental illness, drugs, and alcohol. It is very important for you to get any help you can, and to realize that you cannot possibly be bad enough to deserve this kind of treatment. Maybe you need some other kind of straightening out, but cruelty will not help you.

PEER PRESSURE PROBLEMS

Nearly every young person has peer pressure problems. Your peers are people your own age, and peer pressure is when your peers try to push you into things that you don't want to do. Some peer pressure may be good for you. If the group you hang out with all play games, or know all the makes of cars, or take an interest in clothes and grooming, you may learn a lot from that. But if you know you don't want to get into drugs, sex, liquor, shoplifting, breaking windows, or destroying school property, and the kids around you try to get you to do such things, telling you that if you don't you're a sissy, a wimp, a square, or things like that, then you have bad peer pressure. You are being pushed to do things your family have taught you are wrong.

Maybe you say no for a while, but then you find that saying no means being left by yourself and made fun of all the time. So maybe you go along a little with what the gang wants· you to do. But if you decide things are going too far, you may find it hard to back out. You may in fact be threatened, because the kids are afraid you may rat on them. So your life is miserable. You hate leaving the house, because on the way to school and back you get picked on and bad-mouthed, and you are now really afraid of doing the things they want you to do.

This happens to lots and lots of kids, and the teachers and youth counselors know about it, so if you go to someone and ask for help, you will find yourself talking to someone who understands the fix you are in.

The best thing you can possibly do is to join some youth group where you will have friends and no one will expect you to get in trouble to belong. Church or temple groups and school organizations have marvelous things to do, and people to hang around with who aren't trying to mess you up.

Your parents can be very helpful to you by laying down rules that you have to follow. If the word gets around that your folks are very strict and that they are keeping an eye on you, making you come home early in the evening and pay attention to the way they want you to act, insisting that you hang out with the kind of people they think are good for you, you'll find it a lot easier living in the same neighborhood and the same school as the kids who are trying to drag you down with them. You can ask your parents for help in getting out of that high-pressure peer group.

ASKING FOR INFORMATION

The young people who know the *most* about sex, drugs, and alcohol are the ones who find it easiest to avoid getting into trouble through these things. You can ask your parents for information, and maybe they will prove helpful and ready to talk to you. Or to see that you have books like this to read. But, if they find it hard to talk to you, you can ask for information from other people.

Your school nurse can answer almost any question you have. She may organize small group sessions for discussing sexual problems and for clarifying anything you and others want to know. Or she may prefer to deal with you on an individual basis. After all, nurses at school can be very busy!

In some schools, classes are set up for boys and girls to learn about the basic facts of sex. Often, parents are expected to give their okay to your being in a class like this. The teacher of the class can show your parents the kinds of books you will use, the films that will be shown, and the plan of the course.

Such classes should provide you with not only the facts about sexuality, but other sources where you can get more information. This includes the titles of books, like this one, and the names of organizations that are prepared to help you in case of troubles or other needs.

Having mentioned books as a source of information, we want to urge you to look in the school library or the public library for the good books on sex.

Often, librarians do not have enough money to buy the books on sexual matters that ought to be in their collections. Therefore, you should also get to a good bookstore and see what books they have on this subject. Libraries may get out-of-date. Bookstores have the long-term good books, and they are also very up-to-date.

Books have a great deal to offer you if you want to know the facts about sex. However, there are other good sources that you ought to be able to contact for excellent and important information.

It may be that your family doctor will talk to you about the sexual matters that he or she feels you should know about and understand. You will be able to ask questions during a visit to the doctor's office, and you will receive good information. If your doctor is not sure about some facts, or if you are asking questions that fall into more specialized areas, then you will be told where you might find the best answers.

DOCTOR? COUNSELOR? THERAPIST?

In this chapter, we have used these words for people who can be especially helpful to you with sexual problems. We think, however, that you ought to have a good idea about what such people do, and who they are.

The doctor is usually the physician who practices medicine and who sees you on a regular basis, when you have some kinds of problems, including sexual ones.

He or she will examine you, make necessary tests, and give you the prescriptions you need for your case. You will also be given information and advice that will fit your needs, both for the long run and for solving an actual, present problem.

A counselor may be any person who listens to problems and then helps you to deal with them, maybe to solve them, to put up with them, or to ignore them.

The counselor may be a clergyman who has had training and experience in helping young people with sexual questions or problems. A counselor may also be a highly trained specialist in matters of sexual difficulty. He or she has studied in a university and received a doctor's degree in psychology.

This counselor, who is often called "Doctor," is not a physician, but he or she can provide you with the help you need. You may be referred to such a counselor by your physician when it seems that your questions or problems will take time to deal with and you need a specialist in sexual matters.

Your counselor may give advice, but usually you will be asked questions about yourself, about the kinds of things that interest you or worry you, and about the specific situation that you are now in.

Only after you have had a lot of discussion and have done a lot of talking about yourself will the counselor begin to show you ways of looking at your problems and handling them.

The therapist is the special person who helps you to change how you feel, how you see yourself, and what you do as a sexual person.

Being with a therapist means having almost the same kinds of experiences that you may have with a counselor or with your physician. Usually the "therapy" means a counseling treatment that may lead to a form of cure. This may take longer than what a physician will do, or than what a counselor will plan for you.

When you are advised to visit and talk with one of these specialists, you should feel comfortable about it. You are not expected to do or say anything that will hurt you or anyone else.

You should also understand that whatever you say about your most private and personal feelings and activities will *not* be told to anyone else.

Receiving help of this kind, whether it is "counseling" or "therapy," or a medical consultation, is a safe experience. It is intended to help you and to make your life better. Be glad when it is offered, and take part in it as well as you can. And then follow up with those changes in your ways that will make life more comfortable for you.

10

Contraception—Keeping From Getting Pregnant

There is only one sure way to keep from getting pregnant, if you are a girl. Never let any male put his penis into your vagina!

For a boy, there is only one sure way to avoid getting any girl pregnant. Never put your penis into a vagina!

Whenever a penis gets into a vagina, there is a chance of the girl or woman getting pregnant. Even young girls who were not believed to be ovulating yet, and even older women who thought they had stopped ovulating (as women do when they get older), have been surprised to find that they were pregnant! Those have been unusual cases, but they happen from time to time.

We have made it plain already that this is the only way to be sure of not getting pregnant, but we have to say it again. The reason is that somebody is going to pick up this book and think, "I don't care about all that other stuff. All I want to know about is contraception—how to keep from starting a baby." And that person is going to read just this chapter, and put the book down for good. And we don't want anybody to say we left out the one sure way to avoid pregnancy.

Having made that clear, let's talk about the various methods of contraception, or ways of having sexual intercourse that keep the chances of pregnancy down to *almost* zero.

WHY CONTRACEPTION?

Many people are not ready to become parents and take on the responsibility of raising a child. They do want to have sex, and they want to have that very close and loving feeling that comes with intercourse. They may be married and still not want to have a baby. Perhaps both husband and wife are working hard studying to become doctors, lawyers, teachers, or members of some such profession that requires long training. Or they may both be working and saving money for a bigger house or apartment. Maybe they want to have a few years to travel and see all the places they have dreamed about. They may have decided that being parents isn't for them because they want to give all their lives to some kind of demanding work. There are many reasons for not wanting to have a baby.

But these people can run the risk of getting pregnant because if they did have a baby it wouldn't be a real disaster for them. After all, they are grown up, they are able to make a living, and they are ready to take full responsibility for their actions.

Of course, a young teenager is not in a position to run the risk of pregnancy. But you are curious about contraception, and you deserve to have the best information about it.

SEX WITHOUT INTERCOURSE

Strictly speaking, this is not contraception but avoiding the need for it. But if you have read the rest of this book you know that lovers, whether they have intercourse or not, have many other kinds of sex play that provide arousal, orgasms, and a way to be loving and intimate without risking pregnancy.

You may hear young people saying that this kind of sex is not "the real thing." But the real thing is too darn real for a very young person. The real thing brings the risk of pregnancy and the risk of spoiling all the pleasures that belong to being a young, growing, learning person.

We are not urging you to become involved with another young person in any kind of sexual activity at all, but only telling you what the realities of life are. To the young person who wants to put off all kinds of sex until life has become more certain, we can only say "Bravo!" That is your choice, it is a very sensible one, and you have a whole life before you with all its

Condoms come in one size that fit all erections. They come rolled in the package. When they are unrolled and put on the erect penis, some space must be left at the end for the semen. After the man has ejaculated, his penis becomes softer and he must carefully withdraw from the vagina, holding on to the condom at the open end.

The diaphragm must be prescribed by a doctor since it must be fitted to each individual woman's size. The diaphragm is a nearly flat rubber cup made to fit snugly over the uterus. A sperm-killing jelly or cream is put inside the diaphragm, with a small amount spread over the rim. It must not be removed until at least 8 hours after intercourse.

rewards. There are many religious, ethical, and practical reasons for putting off sex until later.

What are the several kinds of contraception?

CONDOMS

These are shaped like a single finger of a glove and they are usually made of thin rubber. There are some made of animal membrane, and some people think they feel better. But many people who have tried them don't think the difference is important.

A condom can be bought at a drugstore without a doctor's prescription. Nowadays many drugstores display them on self-service racks. The buyer need only to pick up a package and place it on the counter by the cash register. No conversation with the storekeeper is necessary.

Men usually buy the condoms because they are the ones who will use them, but nowadays women buy them too, because they don't want to be caught in a situation where the man has forgotten.

Condoms come in one size. One size fits all erections.

The purpose of the condom is to hold the sperm and keep it from getting into the vagina. The condom comes from the package rolled, so that it looks a little like a small Frisbee. When it is unrolled onto the erect penis—you can't very well put it on unless the penis is erect—it should not be pulled on snugly like a well-fitting sock. Some space should be left at the end for the semen. If this is not done, when the man ejaculates the semen will be forced back down the shaft of the penis. Semen is slippery and it might cause the condom to slide off and let semen into the vagina.

After the man has ejaculated, his penis becomes softer and therefore he must withdraw from the vagina carefully, holding on to the condom at the open end. If he doesn't do that, the condom may slip off into the vagina and spill semen there.

Some condoms come with lubrication on them. If the woman has been aroused and her vagina is wet, this is not so necessary, but there are times when it is a good idea to have lubrication on the condom. One of these times is when the woman is having intercourse for the first time. The lubrication on the condom can make stretching her hymen easier and less uncomfortable.

There are very fancy condoms in odd colors and with textures that are supposed to give the woman more pleasure, but the value of these is doubtful. Plain white condoms made by a known manufacturer are probably the best. Some come with a little nipple or extra space at the end, to catch the semen. The ordinary kind, if they are put on with space left at the end, are just as good.

Condoms are often worn as a guard against venereal disease. For this reason they used to be called prophylactics. They do a good job protecting against infection with gonorrhea, which is caught by letting germs in the vagina get into the penis. Herpes and syphilis, on the other hand, can go from the woman to the man from sores around her genitals discharging infection into tiny cuts and openings in the skin around the man's genitals, so the condom isn't a perfect preventive against V.D.

"Condom" is pronounced "*con-dum.*" You pronounce the *om* to rhyme with "gum."

CONTRACEPTIVE FOAMS, JELLIES, AND CREAMS

Sometimes these are used by themselves, but the best plan is for the woman to use one of these preparations while the man wears a condom.

When using a foam, jelly, or cream, or any other contraceptive, it is only good sense to read the directions on the package and follow them carefully. Many contraceptives have failed to work because people used them carelessly.

All these semiliquids are put into the vagina with dispensers that come with them. The foam works rather like shaving foam, and it goes throughout the vagina and makes a little barrier at the opening of the womb (the cervix). All these preparations have chemicals that kill sperm before they can reach an egg cell.

Some people will say that using these precautions before sex takes all the fun out—but for most people it makes the fun *possible,* because they aren't worrying the whole time about getting pregnant.

The word *spermicidal* appears on the containers of these products. The word means "sperm-killing."

It isn't much use inserting one of these preparations into the vagina *after* sex. By then, some sperm may have gone up into the uterus.

THE PILL

Women who take the pill are prevented by it from producing egg cells. They may still have menstrual periods, however. Some women should not use the pill at all, and for some only certain kinds of birth-control pills are safe. So no one should take a contraceptive pill without getting a prescription from a doctor, who will examine her carefully before prescribing. Although many young women have used the pill with no ill effects, certain bad signs should be watched for. These signs are dizziness, chest pain, shortness of breath, headaches, lumps in the breast, and anything unusual and alarming. If anything like that shows up, the woman must call her doctor. Some makes of pill are taken daily for twenty-one days out of the month, as directed. Users of other brands take one pill every day as long as they are "on" the pill.

THE DIAPHRAGM

The diaphragm must be prescribed by a doctor as it must be fitted to the woman. It comes in several sizes and the fit must be good.

The diaphragm is a nearly flat rubber cup made to fit snugly over the cervix—the opening to the uterus. The doctor shows the woman how to put it into place, which is not difficult but must be done right. During that week she should not count on it for contraceptive protection. A sperm-killing jelly or cream is used with the diaphragm. This is put inside (about a tablespoon) and on the rim (only a small amount) of the diaphragm before it is fitted over the cervix. It must stay in place and not be removed until 8 hours after intercourse.

THE IUD OR INTRAUTERINE DEVICE

"Intrauterine" means within the uterus. The IUD has to be placed inside the uterus with a stringy tail hanging down through the cervix into the vagina. Either a doctor or another professional must insert the IUD, and, when the time comes, remove it. Once in place, it can remain there for months or years.

The IUD is made of somewhat springy plastic or metal. When inserted into the uterus, it expands so that it cannot slip out into the vagina.

The IUD is not a barrier device like the diaphragm or the condom. It does not keep sperm from getting up into the uterus and the fallopian tubes. Sperm can swim up into the fallopian tubes to unite with and fertilize an ovum, or egg cell. But the fertilized ovum cannot attach itself to the uterus wall, so it slips out into the vagina and is expelled from the body of the woman or girl.

Why can't the ovum attach itself to the uterus wall? No one is really sure, but it seems that the IUD mildly irritates the wall of the uterus so that it rejects the ovum.

A doctor has to check the IUD now and then to see that it is in place. Now and then an IUD somehow slips out of the uterus into the vagina. The IUD device is not suitable for all women.

There is a lot of controversy surrounding the IUD so make sure you thoroughly discuss its use with your doctor.

THE SPONGE

The sponge is a fairly new product and it is not yet on sale in all parts of the United States. It is sold in drugstores and no prescription is needed. The girl inserts it into her vagina, where it blocks sperm from entering the uterus. The chemical foam in the sponge kills sperm as well. This is a risky form of contraception and we strongly recommend not using the sponge.

THE NATURAL METHOD

This is also called the "rhythm method" because it is based on the woman's rhythm, or time pattern of ovulation, readiness to conceive, menstruation, and times of not conceiving. The last-mentioned times are called the "safe." By studying her own natural rhythm, the woman learns when the safe time comes during each twenty-eight-day cycle.

The so-called "safe times" are determined by a number of factors. The woman notes on her calendar the date of her last period, takes her temperature, and observes the thickness and thinness of her vaginal mucus to pinpoint her safe times.

No one should use this method without being taught how by professionals who understand it thoroughly.

SOME ABSOLUTELY WRONG IDEAS ABOUT CONTRACEPTION

In the past, before good methods of contraception were developed, people who wanted to avoid pregnancy tried home-made methods, ideas they got from friends and from old-fashioned doctors and nurses. These were not effective methods, and we tell you about them only so that you will know better than to use them.

Coitus interruptus, or interrupted intercourse, is a method people still foolishly rely on. The man withdraws his penis from the vagina before he ejaculates—or tries to. The trouble is that no male can be absolutely sure when he will ejaculate, and that may be too late anyway. Even before he ejaculates, some semen oozes out of his penis, putting live sperm into the vagina. The sperm can migrate to the vagina even if the man withdraws in time and ejaculation occurs near the vagina.

Without thorough training in the natural method, a girl does not know when her "safe" time is. Don't believe her if she says she does!

Some girls have heard that if they urinate right after intercourse it will wash out all the sperm. The trouble is, the sperm is in her *vagina*. If you look at the picture of the female genitals in this book, you will see that the urine does not come out of the vagina, but from the urethral opening, so the sperm is quite safe from it.

Women used to douche—wash out their vaginas with some sort of solution—after intercourse. No good. Contraception must be used *before* intercourse. Whatever you have heard about douching with vinegar and water, Coca-Cola, or anything else, forget it.

Putting a real sperm-killing material into the vagina *after* intercourse won't work either.

Some girls and women have the idea that if they concentrate on not having an orgasm they can't get pregnant. But the sperm and the egg cell don't care whether she has had an orgasm or not.

Having sex standing up doesn't work either.

There—that's enough of ways that don't work. The right method of contraception is one recommended to you by a doctor, clinic, or family-planning center. Don't rely on any other.

WHEN CONTRACEPTION FAILS TO WORK

As we said at the beginning of this chapter, there is no absolutely sure way of preventing conception when people engage in sexual intercourse. Contraceptive methods are very successful for many people who use them very carefully, but there are failures. When contraception fails, the choice is between having the baby or consulting a doctor or clinic and arranging to have the pregnancy aborted. Abortion is not a form of contraception; it is a medical procedure for removing the fertilized egg cell, or the embryo that it has developed into, from the uterus of the woman. This can be done simply and with little pain if it is done very early in the pregnancy. It must be done by a medical specialist in a clinic or hospital. In the earliest weeks of pregnancy, a slim tube can be put through the vagina into the uterus to remove the product of conception by suction. The woman is given a local anesthetic (which does not make her unconscious) and she has little pain. The procedure takes thirty minutes, and after resting an hour or two the woman can go home.

Later in the pregnancy, abortion is more complicated and the woman needs to stay in the hospital overnight.

Many groups and families object to abortion, but the pregnant female is entitled to medical advice on the subject and to have the abortion if she decides to do so. It is best not to make this decision without thorough discussion with the woman's family and/or professional counselors.

Women and girls who decide against abortion must go through pregnancy and give birth to the baby. When keeping the infant is not desired, she can have it offered for adoption. There is a long list of couples waiting to adopt such a baby, and they will give it a home and raise it as their own child. The mother must not expect to see the child or hear about it again.

Sometimes an unmarried girl decides, with her family's agreement, to keep the baby and raise it with her family's support. Or the baby can be raised as another child of her mother and father. This is sometimes done, but since it adds a real burden to the girl's parents, it often turns out to be a poor arrangement.

The choice of marrying the baby's father and beginning a home with him is usually out of the question when the father is too young to take on the responsibility. This arrangement is generally too much for the young parents in the modern world, and it does not provide a solid home for the child.

GETTING THE LATEST INFORMATION

Young people who are having sex, but who don't feel prepared to take on being parents yet, should take advantage of the counseling offered by clinics, health departments, and family-planning agencies. You can get the very latest information there at little or no cost. Physicians and researchers are always working on new ways to provide birth control, hoping to make it cheaper, simpler, and more certain. Don't count on information from a friend. Get it from a professional. To find the right place to go for counseling on contraception in your area, phone your local hospital or public health department. Having the very best information is the best way to prevent problems that may come from sex.

Some of you may be worried that if you go to a clinic or health department for information about contraception, they will inform your parents. As far as we know, at this time, your privacy will be respected and they will not inform them. If you are in doubt about this, you can always check with them first over the telephone before you go.

11

Gay and Straight

"Homosexual" means having sexual desire for persons of one's own sex. There are women who prefer to have sex and love with other women rather than with men. They are sometimes called lesbians, because in ancient times on the Greek island of Lesbos there were homosexual women and a famous woman poet named Sappho who wrote about love between women.

And there are homosexual men, who have sex with other men. You can't pick out the homosexual men in a crowd as easily as you might think—many of them dress quietly and look like other men in the same line of work. Nor are all lesbians easily identified by style or manner.

Nowadays, most homosexuals prefer to be called "gay." It is a bright and brave word, and it tends to reverse the low opinion that people used to have of gays—and that they very often had of themselves. Not long ago, being gay was generally thought of as a kind of sickness or abnormality. Gay people did not march and picket and openly declare their sexual preferences as they do today. The sexual things they did with one another were considered unnatural, although "normal" people did most of the same things more than they used to admit. Very often when "normal" or "straight" people did fellatio and cunnilingus they were ashamed and thought they were being somehow homosexual. Only sexual intercourse was considered normal by the majority of people—in public. A great many straight people are having happier sex lives today because they have accepted much of their own behavior as playful and natural rather than abnormal.

And now the gay people themselves have a better acceptance of themselves than used to be the case. It is still easier to be straight than to be gay, but since the gays began to band together to demand their civil rights, like a number of other minorities, there is less arresting of gays for minor offenses, and they are rarely refused housing because of their sexual preferences, or kept out of higher-salaried jobs that they can do as well as anyone, and so on.

To a larger number of straight people, these changes are not pleasing. People are afraid of seeing the wider acceptance of gays and gay behavior. There is a fear that if gayness is no longer to be called wrong, no longer to be discouraged, a great many more apparently straight people are going to throw their straightness out the window and go gay. Though many more secretly gay people are likely to drop their disguises, it is very doubtful that so-called straight sex is going to go out of fashion.

Psychologists used to be a great deal more certain that they knew the causes of homosexuality than they are today. And they had more assurance about calling the homosexual way an abnormality or a sickness. Some of this change of mind is a result of respect for the political power of gays, but much is also due to the better realization that the subject is much more complicated than it was once thought to be.

Some gays state that they always knew they were attracted to their own sex. Others tell of living through a long period of confusion before settling on a homosexual lifestyle. Some people have a gay phase early in life, then go straight for years, even marrying and having children. In middle age they may return to being gay after the death of husband or wife or after divorce.

BISEXUAL BEHAVIOR

It is not possible to say that there is a line dividing the human race into gay and straight. Men who live as husbands and fathers may have homosexual relations outside marriage, leaving much doubt in the end as to whether they were really homosexuals, who lead straight lives publicly, or straights who just liked a homosexual fling now and then.

People who are known to engage in sex with both men and women, as opportunity allows, are called *bisexuals*. But are they really a separate kind of people? Or are they really just living without any feeling that they must make up their minds?

Psychologists will say of these people (there are women bisexuals as well as men) that they *can* function sexually with either men or women. Not that they don't care, but that they are *able* to have sex either way.

It is rather well established that some people can respond sexually only to one sex or the other. This is most clearly the case with gay men who simply can't have an erection and carry out intercourse with a woman. Such men have sometimes wanted to change, however, and sex therapy has made it possible for a number of them to have intercourse with women after a period of time.

It has also been established that many people who are capable of almost any sexual activity with either sex are living as straights because they want to for moral reasons, religious reasons, because this style of life is more comfortable for them, or something like that.

There is an advantage in regarding one's sexual pattern as one taken by choice. Many straight people will admit that they have had homosexual dreams, unusually strong feelings for certain people of their own sex, and occasional wonderings about what homosexual sex would be like. At times they have caught themselves acting, or sounding, or making a movement or gesture that seems to show a gay tendency. But they know they like straight love and sexual behavior, and they do not trouble themselves about whether they are homosexual or not.

FRIENDSHIP BETWEEN STRAIGHTS AND GAYS

Gay people are capable of friendship, without sexual overtones, with straights of both sexes. This kind of friendship is accepted more and more today, even by conventional people, without suspicion of the straight person's "real" straightness. The self-confident person is not troubled much by suspicions of that sort anyway.

Young men and boys especially are fearful of associating with gays, and when that is so, the association should not be forced. But relations between straight and gay people can almost always be polite and mutually helpful at school and on the job.

YOU DON'T HAVE TO PROVE ANYTHING

If you are a young straight male and someone makes you a homosexual offer, there is no reason for fear or anger unless the offerer is really aggressive or much bigger or older than you. Nine times out of ten, you need only say,

"No, thanks." If the other guy tries to pressure you—"Why not? You *know* you want to."—all you have to say is, "I don't want to talk about this." Don't let the situation make you show anger or violence. Why should you? *He* made the suggestion, not you. You don't have to prove a thing except that you don't want to do anything like that for your own reasons, which you know perfectly well. If you are afraid of the guy, leave. If not, leave or go on talking about other things, as you choose.

Don't let the happening give you the idea that he sees something in you that encourages him to try you. He only did it because he wanted some sex, not because he has any mystical power to read your true character.

IF YOU CAN'T STOP WORRYING

If for some reason you can't stop worrying about whether you are gay or not, you can ask for counseling. Go to your clergyman, your doctor, the school nurse, or whatever adult you trust most, to find where counseling is offered in your area. You can do this whether you have had some homosexual experience or not. Worrying can hurt you; counseling can help you see your problem more clearly and help you to think constructively about it. Remember, whether you are straight or gay, you are a person of value to yourself and to other people.

12

In Conclusion

The real purpose of this book is to make people's lives happier and to offer a better understanding of sex.

Parents, most of them, want their children to grow up and have good lives, with love and companionship. And mutual pleasure with the persons they love. If parents try to scare their children away from accidents that really can happen, and do happen every day—well, you can see why they might want to do that!

At your present stage in life, you may not want to get into sex yet. You know that for yourself you are happier learning about it a little at a time, learning about yourself and other people in your life in an unhurried way. You have too many other things going on right now to try to take on grown-up sex. You like to think about that as something for later on.

Don't let anyone pressure you into going faster than your own sweet pace. It's your life, so be sure to enjoy it each day as you live it—as well as in your dreams and plans for your future.

Goodbye, good luck, and have a wonderful life!

Index